Meditations
for Miracles

The Keys to Life Mastery

By
Diane L. Ross

CDs by Diane L. Ross

1. Instant Meditation
2. Meditation for Making Contact With The Other Side
3. Meditation for Pain Relief
4. Soul-ly Positive (A Meditation for Comfort and Well Being)
5. Self-Hypnosis to Stop Smoking
6. Self-Hypnosis for Stress Reduction & Relaxation
7. Self-Hypnosis for Weight Loss
8. Meditation for Communication With Your Spirit Guides

More CD titles are listed on page 375.

**For more information or to purchase, go to
www.dianeross.com or
email Diane at diane@dianeross.com.**

Dedication

This book is dedicated to the
Divine spark in each of you.
Thank you for sharing your light.

10 - 30 - 17

Dear Jennifer,

It is a pleasure
being even a small part
of your path!

Love & blessings,
Diane

Contents

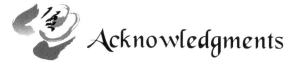

Acknowledgments

I would like to thank my husband, Randy Parsley, for his continual support and encouragement during the process of writing and publishing this book. I would also like to thank our son, Peter Parsley, for his wonderful understanding and compassion; my exceptional parents: Marilynn Brooks Ross, who crossed over to the other side in 2006, and my father Ray Ross, who passed away in 1997; my brother Jeff Ross, who made his transition in 1966; my brother Greg Ross, who passed over in 2007; my sister and dearest friend, Theresa Ross Parrish, who continues to share her insights and wisdom and whose editing expertise added greatly to the quality of this book; and my brother Ron Ross, who so graciously provided the magnificent art for the cover of this book.

I would also like to thank Alexia Dawson, Kathryn Dibernardo, Marilyn Hunte, Barbara Konits, and Crosby Stapleton for their help in typing and editing.

Special thanks to editor Ingrid Powell for her amazing brilliance, and to my friend, Joleta Ross, whose talents contributed immeasurably to this production.

Thanks to Durga Ma of Phoenix, Arizona, whose loving teachings continue to inspire me.

There are many, many others, who have influenced my life in positive ways and indirectly provided support and enthusiasm for this project.

Thank you all for being miracles in my life.

Introduction

This is a book of daily meditations. These meditations are designed to help you create miracles in your life.

A Course in Miracles defines "miracle," as a shift in perception. If you have ever changed your perception, you know how difficult that is, a true miracle! Perception is changed, the mind is changed, one thought at a time; that's why daily meditation is crucial.

These meditations are written in poetic prose so that each sentence is savored. Some of the ideas may seem foreign, and some of the ideas may seem ordinary, but in combination will hopefully produce the extraordinary in your life.

Read the book in the way that serves you best. You may want to read the meditations by date, or you may want to flip through the book to the meditation the universe "wants" you to read. You can't read it wrong!

The main thing is to read with *your heart*.

Let the insights penetrate your heart, so that you can have a perceptual shift, and miracles can occur in *your* life!

It's best to read no more than one meditation per day. Reading more may be tempting, but since each meditation contains a specific concept, reading more than one a day may not give your heart a chance to integrate the material.

Meditation may be an exercise for the mind, but its gifts are received in the heart.

Balance occurs when the mind, the heart, and the body are in alignment. That's when you are in balance with the divine and are able to manifest miracles!

Read with your heart, and may many miracles manifest in your life!

Love and blessings,

Diane

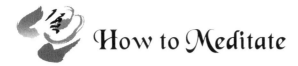

How to Meditate

Meditation is the process of focusing your attention on a single object or idea. To practice meditation, sit down and get the body comfortable. Close your eyes. Put your attention on your breath as you inhale and exhale. Don't try to control the breath, just become aware of it.

When a thought pops into your mind, simply become aware of it, mentally toss it into a river and watch it flow away from you. Then put your attention on the area about an inch above your eyebrows, in the center of your forehead (your "third eye"). When a thought enters your mind, toss it in the river and watch it float away. You might think, "Oh, that's a thought," and then focus on your breath.

Keep alternating your focus between your breath and your third eye. This process may sound simple, and it is, but its effects are profound. Focusing on the third eye activates your spiritual energies and connects you with your inner divinity. Focusing on the breath is an ancient technique that has been used for centuries.

With practice, you will become aware of your thoughts. You will realize that your thoughts are *not* you. This is the first step in learning to focus your thinking. This process also helps keep your attention in the present moment, where creativity, miracles, and life itself, begins.

It's best to meditate at least once a day, preferably in the morning before leaving your house, as this sets the tone for the entire day. Twenty minutes is the optimal time to spend in one sitting. If possible, also meditate in the afternoon and once again before bedtime.

If this seems daunting, just meditate when you can for as long as you can. Even three minutes can be effective. A little is better than nothing.

For optimal results, listen to a recorded meditation such as Diane's "Instant Meditation" CD to get you started. This will guide you through the process effortlessly. Practice with the recording until you have learned it sufficiently to do on your own. Thereafter, listen to the recording as needed for reinforcement.

The meditations that follow may be more aptly described as contemplations. They are designed to be "meditated," or contemplated upon, but for the most part are not techniques in themselves. They are designed to shift your perception, stretch your mind, and open your heart to the wisdom that is already in your soul. It is only through quieting the chatter of the mind that the holiness of your soul is revealed.

 # A Note About God

The term God has been used throughout the book, but it has not been defined. I would not presume to define God. God is different for everyone, and part of your job is to come to terms with what God means to you. If you have trouble with the term God, substitute whatever works for you; love, the divine, endless creativity, infinite wisdom, unending goodness, or use your own definition.

In this context, one thing that we all may agree upon is that God is good!

The Mystery of Co-Creation

Learning to *direct your attention* is one of the most important skills you can master.

It is through directing your attention that you learn to control your energies and assume your role as co-creator.

Co-creation is not as mysterious as it sounds.

Co-creation begins with aligning your individual energies with the ever-present divine energies flowing through you.

This alignment begins by directing your attention, which is the foundation of co-creation.

Any change (creation) you want to make in your life begins with a thought.

To manifest change, focus your attention on your thoughts.

Learning this process is where time comes in.

Time allows you the opportunity to practice.

If it weren't for the element of time, you wouldn't need to practice focusing your attention because your thoughts would manifest immediately.

It is how you direct your attention through time that allows you to co-create and achieve your goals.

As you practice focusing your attention you are practicing the first step of co-creation.

Practice, and the mystery of co-creation reveals itself quite naturally!

෨ ෨ ෨

Fear is Forgetting to Trust

Sometimes your job is to listen to the "quiet."
Hear the stillness.
To be *aware* of stillness, *you* must be still.
Being still invites richness into your life that you cannot imagine when in a hurried, rushed state.
If you are not familiar with this deep, inner quiet, you may fear it.
The fear creates activity, which destroys the stillness.
Let yourself experience the fear.
Go *through* the state of not trusting, not knowing.
Go through the unknowing and find the spark of light, the spark of God's love within you.
Let in the glow of God's love and allow the light to become brighter.
Breathe in the light until it fills your entire being!
Now listen to the quiet.
Let the stillness permeate every aspect of your being.
Hear no sound.
Let the stillness heal you from the inside out, on all levels of your being.
Notice how *simple* everything is.
Notice how *powerful* the stillness is.
Notice how *full* this stillness is.
Notice as you begin to *trust the stillness*, the fear is gone.
There is no fear in the stillness of God's love.
And should you forget and become afraid, simply be still and breathe in the light of love.

Love is Nature's Antidepressant

The energy of love contains all the chemicals your brain needs in order to feel the best you can possibly feel.

Pharmaceutical antidepressants don't make you feel good; they simply keep you from feeling really bad.

Cultivating love guarantees that you will feel good.

Focus on love and the side effects are enormously positive.

There are many ways to cultivate love.

Think of something that brings you joy and focus on it, breathe it in.

Breathe the feeling of joy into your lungs.

Imagine the joy traveling from your lungs into your bloodstream, filling your entire body.

When you feel this joy throughout your entire being, notice that you can't separate joy from love.

Notice how joy, bliss, and happiness merge.

Notice that you don't need to focus these emotions on any particular thing, place, or person.

You can experience the profound feelings of love within.

Love does not come from an outside source.

As you cultivate this divine love, your inner source of strength grows.

This strength cannot be diminished by any outside source.

As you tap into this inner wellspring of God's love, it gets stronger.

Cultivate love, and sadness doesn't have room to exist within you.

Cultivate love – nature's antidepressant!

Doubt is a Certainty

It is *certain* that you will experience doubt.
Are you doing the right thing?
Are you on the right path?
Are you making the right decision?
Doubt is simply *not knowing.*
There is nothing wrong with not knowing.
You are here to learn.
If you already knew everything, you wouldn't be here.
Becoming aware that you don't know is no reason to stop what you are doing.
After all, you are going to be doing something.
Even doing nothing is doing something.
Doing nothing doesn't stop doubt.
Doing nothing keeps you stagnant, stuck in "not knowing."
It's better to take action and have doubt than to stay stuck.
You're going to experience doubt regardless of what you do or don't do, so take action!
When you experience doubt, simply say, "Okay, this is doubt."
Don't claim it.
Keep it in perspective.
You are not doubt; you are *experiencing* doubt.
When you recognize doubt for what it is, you take away its power over you.
When you don't know, you open the door to knowing.
It is only when you open the door to knowing that you can receive knowledge.
Doubt is the first step to knowing!

Harmony Is Your Natural Tune

Harmony is the gift you receive when you release the mind's confusion.

The mind's confusion affects your entire being.

Regardless of how intense your confusion may be, when you surrender to the divine, harmony is the ultimate outcome.

Harmony is the natural result of being in tune with the divine.

It's not that you *create* harmony: You uncover it.

Harmony naturally underlies every aspect of your being.

Lift each layer of discord, notice it, and allow it to float away.

The rich harmonies of your own personal resonance sound with clarity and vibrancy, moving the universe as no other sound can.

Appreciate your harmony.

You are the *only one* who vibrates in this exact manner.

Your harmony is as unique and beautiful as you are.

The negatives that you claim as your own are false and create discord in the mind.

Who you really are on a soul level is in total harmony with the divine.

Confusion exists in the mind, *not in the soul.*

Let go of the mind's confusion and allow yourself to be in tune with divine harmony.

The Gift of Your Body

Your body is a gift.

Regardless of its condition, your job is to honor it.

Your body is the physical means through which your soul can express itself.

Ask yourself, "How do I want to use my body?"

To express creativity?

To show love?

Does it serve you, or do you serve it?

Does it help you achieve what you want, or does it distract you?

Do you give it rest, care, and proper maintenance?

Or do you abuse and exhaust it?

You don't need to inhabit an optimally healthy body in order to achieve your goals.

There are many souls with poorly functioning bodies who have learned to utilize them successfully.

In fact, most people have bodies that will never be considered optimal.

The body is biodegradable, so that it can return to the earth when you leave it.

Honor the body's gift while you have it, as you will never have it again.

Part of your lessons may involve learning to adjust as your body declines.

What changes have you made as your body changes?

What has your body taught you?

What have you learned by having the gift of your body?

The Elixir of Life: Sleep

Sleep is a requirement of the body, the mind, and the soul.

Without sleep, it is impossible for your energies to come into alignment and balance with divine energies.

The body, mind, and soul need rest in order to rejuvenate and heal.

The term "running ragged" refers to times in which you move so quickly that your energies don't have a resting period.

Your energies literally become "ragged": scattered and inefficient.

You become unable to focus.

Sleep is the dimension in which information regarding all aspects of your life can be received.

It allows your consciousness to experience expanded states not possible to achieve any other way.

It allows your soul to integrate lessons learned throughout the day.

During sleep you work out problems, receive help from your angels and guides, and get inspiration for implementing ideas into the physical.

During sleep you may be given symbols that can validate your progress.

Honor the natural cycles of rest and life's struggles will be fewer.

Sleep is truly the elixir of life, a gift from the heavens.

Accessing God

You may think that in order to experience the love of God, you have to go *outside* yourself.

What you don't realize is that this golden grail is within you.

It's not a matter of going outside; it's a matter of going inside.

The tranquility, peace, love, and comfort are already inside, waiting for you to access them.

God's love must be within you in the first place, or you wouldn't know how to *recognize it.*

That's why the scriptures exhort you to be still, to meditate, and to know God.

When the caterpillar transforms into the butterfly, it first attaches itself to a safe place and then becomes totally still.

During this time of extreme stillness, the last instar, or exoskeleton, of the caterpillar is shed.

Inside this instar is the chrysalis.

After the chrysalis is exposed, the rest of the metamorphosis takes place; again, *inside.*

The result of this mysterious transformation emerges after a period of stillness to reveal the fascinating beauty of the butterfly, which existed in some other form on the *inside the whole time*!

It is only through stillness that this transformation can take place.

This deep inner change is more than a metaphor.

The love of God is inside you, waiting to be discovered through stillness, so it can do its transformative work.

Be still and access the God *within you.*

Let Nature Help Manifest Your Ideals

Look at the different forms of life.

See them as individual units of energy.

Notice how they are all perfectly functioning and uniquely suited to their tasks.

Each bird, each beetle, each butterfly has the perfect design for its job.

Each creature is so focused, so intense, yet so natural, its manifestation seems totally effortless.

That's why it is important to look to nature for guidance.

How can *you learn* to focus your energies so completely?

Notice how the creatures seem to perform effortlessly.

If they need to be fierce to defend themselves or their families, they experience it in every cell of their bodies.

If they sing a song of joy, they sing it with abandon, for all to hear.

There are no half measures in nature.

The creatures perform with magnificent focus and intention.

A blade of grass has only one intention: To grow.

Become aware of *your intention*.

What do *you* want to manifest?

The first step in manifesting your intention is becoming aware of *what that is!*

Become aware.

Focus your attention.

Meditate.

Practice.

∽ ∽ ∽

Become a Tuning Fork for the Divine

Listen.
Within you is your own unique song.
When you become still, you can hear this music.
This is your special sound, a sound that only you can hear, and only you can make.
Once you are in tune with its frequency, you can receive information that you are divinely designed to receive.
Your individual vibration is different than any other.
It is sacred and holy and cannot be duplicated.
That is why the essence of your life must be honored.
You cannot create life, but you can nourish it.
Part of the mission of your soul is to align all of your energies to this inner vibration.
When you are able to sing this song in harmony, your mission will manifest.
Listening and being still allows you the opportunity to learn your song, to become familiar with its melody.
How can you sing your song unless you know its tune?
Even as you learn the tune, you are required to practice.
That's why each life is so important.
No individual vibration can ever be duplicated.
Your job is to become a tuning fork for the divine, so that God's energy can resonate through you.
Be still.
Listen.
Practice your song.

The Foundation of Co-Creation

Begin each day with, "Thank you, God. I love you."

Turn each distracting thought to gratitude and love.

As this becomes your focus, your entire day will resonate with holy intentions.

When you begin each day with these intentions your life will begin to change.

Your energies will align with the divine.

Your thoughts, feelings, and emotions will naturally come back to these holy intentions throughout the day.

If you get upset, simply bring yourself back to these sacred thoughts of gratitude and love.

Gratitude and love form the foundation of co-creation.

Love of God is the essence of all love.

Meditate on these holy thoughts and let them become part of you.

As your energies align with divine energies, you become more aware, more conscious.

Your intuition and psychic abilities will increase.

You'll become aware of subtle energies and how to cope more easily with the outside world.

This is truly the path to wisdom.

Use gratitude and love as your cornerstone, your foundation, and you will naturally evolve into a co-creator.

∽ ∽ ∽

The Void

Sometimes you get no answers.

Sometimes there seems to be no solution to a problem, circumstance or relationship.

That is the time to be with your unknowing, to sit with it, and to feel it.

Accepting your "not knowing" and your state of emptiness are as important as knowing and being full.

You must be aware of what these states *are not*, in order to know what they *are*.

Experiencing contrast is a necessary part of being human.

It is especially important to experience emptiness, and at the *same time*, understand that this is a *temporary* state.

Emptiness will always be filled; not knowing will always turn to knowing.

It is not only *natural* to be empty; it is *imperative*.

You cannot be filled unless you are empty.

Think of empty as quiet and still, and the void can become filled.

When you quit trying to fill the emptiness yourself, the divine will fill it for you.

~ ~ ~

Your Personal Power

Personal power is the ability to *choose* which aspects of yourself you want to manifest.

Do you want to manifest kindness, integrity, and steadfastness?

Or do you want to manifest hostility, resentment, and impatience?

Real empowerment occurs when you become conscious enough to choose *what to express* and *how to express it.*

What are your ideals of yourself?

How would you *like* to be?

You have the ability to choose your personal expressions of who you are.

You must first become aware, moment-by-moment, of who you want to be, how you want to feel, and what you want to express.

Then, moment -by -moment, you move closer to being, feeling, and expressing your highest ideals.

This is truly the path to personal power.

When you can consciously choose how to use your energies, you are powerful.

When you align your energies with divine energies, you become a true co-creator.

If God is love and you choose to align your energies with God, then with what are you aligning your energies?

What are you expressing?

What powers do you have?

~ ~ ~

Relax in God's Love

Let yourself experience the reassurance that you are being guided, cared for, and adored on all levels of your being.

Feel the divine love.

Let it flow through your body like fragrant mists of everlasting light.

Feel its presence within you now, and know that it is always with you.

As you clean out the cobwebs of inner doubt, replace them with gold-spun threads of divine guidance.

Let prayer be the food your mind feasts upon.

Let love be the energy that guides every cell in your body.

Let each atom smile with joy as you allow positive energy to radiate in ever-widening circles from within you.

Let love be what powers your soul and you will never run out of energy.

It is not through suffering that you develop the soul; it is through joy.

See God in spite of your pain.

Focus on good, regardless of circumstances.

Allow your gifts to shine through tragedy.

Relax in God's love.

〜 〜 〜

Gratitude Creates Miracles

The path to God is paved with gratitude.

Gratitude opens the doorway through which the Holy Spirit enters.

When you are thankful for even the smallest thing, miracles begin to happen.

Gratitude opens your heart to receive miracles.

Let God use you to manifest His grace.

Begin your gratitude wherever you are.

If you can see, open your eyes and find one thing for which you can be grateful.

It may be the flash of a butterfly's wings or the comfort of a familiar face.

If you can hear, listen to the sounds around you.

Be thankful for the sound of the phone's ring, a loved one's voice, or footsteps across the floor.

If you can walk, journey outside to appreciate nature's pleasures.

Experience the connection you have with the earth.

Treasure the sensation of air on your skin, the warmth of light and the coolness of dark as the sun plays across the skies.

If you can eat, be thankful for the taste of pure, sweet water in your mouth, how soft it feels as it caresses your tongue and throat.

Think of all the many, many wonderful things you have to be grateful for *now*, in *this moment*.

Thank God *now*, and watch your life change.

Don't delay delight!

Each thought of gratitude brings you closer to God.

∾ ∾ ∾

What the #%&*! Are You Thinking?

Begin to change your thinking about every *perceived* negative aspect of your life.

Change, "I'm nervous about," to "I'm excited about."

Change, "I'm afraid," to "I have the chance to *be brave* regarding…"

Change feelings of inadequacy into feelings of having the opportunity to *rise to a higher level.*

Catch your thinking before it has a chance to bring you down into the morass of negativity.

If you're already in a dark state, think of one positive thing in your life until it becomes magnified into the central focus of your being, until it fills you with light.

Let this light permeate every atom in your being until all darkness and negativity have gone.

Practice this exercise until a negative thought can't penetrate your being.

Train your brain.

Train you brain to work for you, not against you.

If you are fostering negative thoughts, you're giving your brain a diet of chemicals that will only feed it more negativity.

Give your brain a diet of positive thoughts so that it will produce positive chemicals.

This will not only make your mind healthy, it will make your entire being healthy.

Your *thinking* is a *tool* for your soul's development!

Change your thinking and your thinking *will change your life.*

Watching Miracles Manifest

When you really want something, no matter what it is, imagine that you *already have it*.

Think of yourself as *already* possessing it.

Perhaps you want a romantic relationship; a child; a house in the country; a new car; to achieve your ideal weight; union with the divine - see yourself as *already having it*.

Experience how it *feels* to have it.

How does having this change you?

How are you different now?

In your mind's eye, step into these changes, step into this different you.

Notice that you have the ability to feel different *now*, in this moment.

Notice how your energy has shifted.

Become aware of how your thinking has changed.

Notice how different you feel emotionally.

Now *thank God* for these changes.

Thank God that you truly do have what you want.

It may seem like an act of pretense, but when you behave as if you already have your desires and thank God for them, you *align your energies to receive them*.

Act as if you have your desires *now*, and be *thankful*.

Don't think of them as something you "want," or you'll always keep them in the future, out of reach.

Be thankful in *this moment* for these wonderful treasures and watch the miracles manifest!

Use Your Body for Divine Glory

Don't forget to honor the body.

Don't forget that you chose your body as a *vehicle* for developing *your soul*.

The body allows you to experience a concrete reality, which would otherwise be unavailable to the soul.

You can grow through this physical experience in ways that accelerate your soul's development.

Since you have *chosen* the physical avenue, it's important that you *honor* all its aspects.

Your thoughts and your emotions affect this glorious physical tool, as does how you treat it in other ways, such as exercise and diet.

As you learn to honor the body, you learn to honor the soul.

If you can relate to your body as your partner, and take care of this partner, you life will naturally be enhanced.

You want your partner to be healthy and experience joy, but you don't want to overindulge it.

You want to enhance each other's lives equally with joy and compassion.

You *came here* to experience the physical world and you must remember to cherish it.

Work *with* your body.

Don't enslave it and don't let it enslave you.

Notice how differently it responds when you allow love to flow through it.

Let it glow with the light of your love, as you glow with the light of God's love.

Use your body for divine glory and enlist it in your job of creating miracles.

Let Your Soul Hear God

Do you listen to God every day?

How do you listen?

How do you still the chatter in your mind so the soul can hear?

Meditate.

Yes, but what does that mean?

It means giving the mind a job.

The mind is *not* what hears God.

If you give the mind a job, it finally gets tired and gives up; in that instant after the mind gives up, the soul has the opportunity to hear God.

Why not give the mind's chatter to God in the first place?

Willingly, lovingly, joyfully offer your energy to God and let Him use it as He wills.

Once you surrender to the divine, you are free to listen, to hear, and to receive.

Once you let go of your own will, you are open to receive God's will.

You are not giving up – *you are giving to God.*

Divine guidance comes to you as you release your own guidance.

Surrendering to the Divine is a process.

You get better with practice.

The more you give, the easier it is to receive.

The more you receive, the easier it is to practice.

Ever wonder why meditation is called a "practice"?

Practice surrendering your mind to God and learn to listen with your soul.

You Don't Co-Create Alone

Are you always in a hurry?

Do you rush from one thing to another?

Rushing around may put a false sense of importance and urgency in your life.

What is your greatest priority?

How do you want to feel about yourself?

What kind of example do you want to be for others?

How are you choosing to spend your time?

How have you arranged your life in order to fulfill your dreams?

What choices have you made that allow you to achieve your goals?

Remember, they are *your life* and *your choices,* but you are not alone.

You can call on your guides, your angels, and divine guidance to help you.

When you realize that *this is co-creation*—you and divine guidance working together—it will make it easier for you to create miracles.

You must, however, take the time, or *make the time*, in your life to receive this guidance.

Working alone is not only extremely difficult; it is also unnecessary.

Decide what miracles you want to create, and slow down so that you can receive help co-creating them.

∽ ∽ ∽

Meditation on Crossing Over

Don't let death's journey frighten you.

Death is only scary because of superstitions and gory stories that have been passed down through the ages.

As you approach your time to pass into death's realm, you can make it easier by letting go of regrets, sorrows, resentments, and angers.

Make the decision to *forgive yourself* and *others*.

Allow your consciousness to expand.

Become aware of your guardian angels and loved ones who have already crossed over, waiting to guide you on your journey.

Let your energies expand into this glorious realm, getting closer and closer to the light.

Experience how good it feels to let go of the past and journey into the future of endless joy.

Don't regret leaving anyone or anything behind; in truth, you're not leaving them for long.

They will join you soon enough, when it's their time to journey.

And you will be there to *help them* on their way, just as others are there to help you now.

Expand your consciousness and allow your energies to join with the brilliant light of God's love.

You are always safe in God's love, the true heaven, which is your destiny.

Go now, free, loved, loving, and safe in God's arms.

Follow the light into the realms of everlasting joy, taking with you blessings and love, now and forever.

Practice these steps so that when your time comes you will be comfortable with the process of making the transition.

Create Your Own Heaven

It is up to you to create *your own heaven*.

All the tools and gifts to create this heaven are already within you.

Part of your mission is to discover these tools and gifts and learn how to use them.

You are like seeds of God planted here on earth.

You already possess everything to express your brightest potential.

It is up to you to decide how to use the sun's energy, how to use the soil's nutrients, how to use the life-giving rain.

Do you choose to look toward the sun and smile in gratitude?

Do you choose to thank the earth for its nurturing forces?

Do you choose to bless the rain in thanksgiving?

Do you choose to honor whatever your inner gifts are, in spite of where you may have been planted?

You have unique inner treasures waiting to blossom.

Each blossom is exquisitely different, yet essential to the world's evolution.

Honor your gifts.

There are none like them anywhere else in the universe!

As you allow your treasures to unfold, you create heaven in this world.

You are here to nourish the heaven that is already within you, to cultivate it and to rejoice in its growth.

No One is Holier than You

There are infinite ways to experience God.

Since God is the energy within all things, all things that you experience can lead to God.

You can smell a flower and know God.

You can feel the cool waters of a rushing stream and know God.

You can taste a berry and know God.

You can know God by going within yourself.

You can know God by *choice* or by *accident*.

You can spend an entire lifetime seeking the Divine, or it can happen in a nanosecond.

There is no right way or wrong way to know God.

God is pulsing through your veins and looking through your eyes at this very moment.

No one is holier than you!

Your mission is *to know* this.

Your job is *to live* this knowledge.

As you become aware of divine presence, become aware that it is within you, without you – everywhere and everywhere there isn't a where.

Simply be open and *trust*.

The light of God is within you.

No one is holier than you.

You are a Prism of Love

Don't ever stop yourself from loving.

Even if the object of your love is an ex-husband, an ex-wife, a former lover, a deceased parent or child - always *allow the love to flow.*

Love is a brilliant energy, one that serves only good.

Your job is to let the light of love shine *through you.*

Don't try to control or direct it.

Be a vehicle for its light.

Think of yourself as a prism.

Your job is to be a clear channel and allow the light to shine, unobstructed, through you.

The clearer your prism, the more brilliantly the light can shine through.

Seek clarity.

Ask the Divine to help you let go of what blocks the light, be it anger, jealousy, resentment, or impatience.

As you let go of these blocks, the light shines ever brighter through you, illuminating not only you, but everything around you.

If you *try* to stop loving another, you create an energetic knot within your prism.

The light not only gets blocked from flowing outward, but it also can't return to you.

When you block the flow of love to another, you block the flow of love to yourself.

Allow the light of love to flow through you and shine ever outward.

Be a clear prism and let God's light shine through you.

What is Your Truth?

Is there an absolute truth?

Is there an absolute right and an absolute wrong?

If you seek connection to your inner truth, outer truths become more apparent.

Your job is to express the truth of who you are.

That's why knowing yourself is so important.

That's why it's so important to become still.

Is there such a thing as absolute light?

When you allow the real you to shine, there is no end to the light!

Questions of relativity become insignificant.

One light is no more meaningful than another.

You are as extremely significant as all others.

You are a unique treasure in the eyes of God.

As you get closer to discovering your inner treasures, you become closer to discovering the treasures of others.

As you appreciate the inside, it becomes easier to appreciate the outside.

As your appreciation grows, your treasure grows.

Kindness, love, and appreciation begin *within*.

Let that be the beginning of your truth.

Holy Evolution

There is no end to learning and acquiring wisdom.

Learning doesn't end because evolution doesn't end.

Wisdom doesn't end because there is always more to know at each level of growth.

As you learn more, joy grows.

As joy grows, trust grows.

As trust grows, love grows.

The quality of your love reflects this holy evolution.

Your ability to resonate with divine energy determines your ability to love.

Imagine tapping into eternal, divine bliss!

The beauty is that this is an unending process, yet a process that you can tap into *now,* this very instant!

Each instant is a moment of bliss in eternity.

You don't need to wait for some time in the future when you will have "arrived."

Your time for bliss is *now, here, in this second!*

Allow yourself to resonate with the living earth, the flowers and the trees.

Do you think they are "waiting" to experience joy?

They are experiencing joy as you are reading this!

Each moment of their lives is joyful because they are fulfilling their divine purpose.

There is nothing you need to "do" in order to experience this bliss; simply step into it now!

There is no end to this bliss, as there is *no end to you.*

You are eternal, as are wisdom and bliss.

You are in the midst of eternal bliss right now.

Acknowledge it, feel it, experience it.

There is no end to it and there is no end to your holy evolution.

❦ ❦ ❦

The Universe is in Divine Order

Everything is in divine order.

At this moment, everything exists as it is *supposed to*.

Every bud is opening on schedule.

Every wisp of wind is blowing as it should.

Every cloud is forming by design.

Every star is in its place in heaven.

You are exactly where you are supposed to be in this eternal moment.

Divine order exists within you just as it exists outside of you.

Don't allow yourself to be fooled by what appears to be chaos.

You only see it as chaos because you haven't learned to see the order in it.

Within chaos is an order waiting to emerge.

Chaos is an illusion you must overcome in order to achieve the next level of cosmic consciousness.

Let your heart beat in unison with the rhythm of the universe and you will experience no fear.

Fear allows the illusion of chaos to continue.

Release yourself from the illusion and put yourself into the arms of peace.

Peace and order are waiting, always, to embrace you.

Allow yourself to be lifted into their loving arms, where divine order exists.

You and the universe are in divine order *now*.

Your Soul's Reflection

Trust that *every person* in your life has *profound value*.

Every person in your life has extreme importance, regardless of how small you think his or her role is.

Think of each person you encounter as being a reflection of your soul.

Each reflection is designed to teach you something about yourself.

Each reflection has the potential to help you learn about the world.

Each reflection is a world in itself.

Each reflection mirrors the Divine, just as you do.

As you appreciate the value of each individual soul, your ability to be a vehicle for light grows.

Trust that each and every soul in your life is there for you to honor and love.

Just as each soul is a reflection of you, you are a reflection of it.

Your light makes theirs brighter, and their light makes yours brighter.

Each soul reflects each soul, yet is profoundly unique.

As you value the light in others, your own light shines brighter.

෨ ෨ ෨

Be Fearless

Fear comes when you forget God is taking care of you.

It is natural to forget, from time to time, how important you are to Him.

As you are distracted from the present moment, you open yourself to uncountable fears and worries.

You forget that what you really are can *never be hurt*.

Fear pulls you away from this knowledge.

Fear pulls you away from this light and into the darkness.

The only way this can happen, however, is if you forget your true nature as a *totally and completely loved soul*.

You may forget that God's love for you is the most powerful force in the universe.

You may forget that His light always overcomes darkness.

You are a prism for that light.

As you bring yourself back from your fears, back into the present moment, you allow the light to shine through and eliminate the shadows of your doubts.

Don't "try."

Don't "work" at it.

Simply bring yourself back to the center of your being and let God shine through you.

When you are in that center, there is no fear.

You are living within God's perfection.

Remember that God is taking care of you.

Be fearless.

∾ ∾ ∾

Let Your Miracles Begin Now!

What do you want to achieve on *all levels of your being:* Physical, emotional, and spiritual?

Do you want health?

Abundance?

Peace of mind?

Wisdom?

Security?

Union with the Divine?

Imagine having whatever you want.

Imagine seeing the sights you would see, hearing the sounds you would hear, feeling the emotions you would feel!

Now *thank God* for manifesting these in your life.

Continue this practice as often as possible until it becomes your natural state.

Thank God for your unlimited resources.

Let every cell in your body vibrate with the joy of fulfilling your dreams.

Notice how much energy you have!

Notice how good you feel!

Notice how confident, vibrant, and alive you are!

This is your *natural state!*

This is the state you came here to manifest!

The more you practice manifesting this state, the more real it becomes.

The more real it becomes, the more you attract into your life what you want to achieve!

Begin this instant.

Feel it now, think it now, and see it now!

Let your miracles begin *now!*

༄ ༄ ༄

Trust the Universe

Trust.

Trust that as the winds blow, as the night comes, as the stars shine, the universe supports you with the essence of its being.

Trust that as your body knows how to convert the air you breathe into its life-giving force, your place on this holy planet is sacred.

Your place is beyond your personal space; your place is *every place.*

Your place is as large as your consciousness can reach, and since your consciousness has no limits, there are no limits to your place.

Where do you exist?

Where are your limitations?

How have you limited yourself?

Are your limitations large or small?

What would you be if you had no limitations at all?

What would you think?

What would you believe?

What would you dream?

Trust that the universe supports these dreams.

Your wildest inclinations are fulfilled as you let go of self-imposed limits and expand your consciousness into the trust of universal love.

You are as important as the winds, the night and the stars. Trust!

Choosing From Love

When you are uncertain about what to do, how to think, or how to be, focus your attention on something you love.

Put your attention on something you adore.

It could be a person, a tree, a song, an animal, a place… anything.

Find something you love and allow your energy to focus there.

Let the energy flow from you to this object.

Allow the love to get as strong as you can possibly make it.

Experience how good it feels to let this profound energy flow through every atom in your being.

Now, bring your attention back to that about which you were uncertain.

Notice the perceptual shift that has occurred as you think about this.

It's so much easier to choose from this vantage point.

Even if you don't know what to do, what to think, or how to be, you know what *not* to do, what *not* to think, how *not* to be.

By eliminating half of your options, achieving clarity is easier.

When you allow the energy of love to flow through you, all decisions are easier.

◦◦ ◦◦ ◦◦

Aspects of God

Think of every person you encounter as incorporating an aspect of God.

Each person has a unique aspect of the Divine that can only manifest through that individual.

Seek always to honor that individual *and* His aspect in them.

True joy comes when you allow yourself to recognize God in all things.

This is the joy of union, of unending expansion and inclusion at the *same time*.

This boundless joy is the spark of creation that resides in you.

Your job is to uncover it while you still exist in your physical body.

As you polish the mirror of your soul, the reflection of this divine aspect becomes brighter.

As you discover the bliss of your own divine nature, it becomes easier to recognize in others.

As you recognize God in all things, the importance of honoring each individual becomes certain.

Which aspects of God will you encounter today?

Don't Limit Your Love, Expand It!

Notice how it feels to be in love.

You possess infinite strength, courage, and resilience.

As you experience this love, notice how healthy your body feels.

Your breath is fuller and easier.

Your muscles move effortlessly.

Even your thinking is clearer.

Now take this love and direct it towards God.

When you direct it towards God, exactly where are you directing it?

Is it one particular place?

How can that be?

Is God in one place?

What exists in all the other places where God is not?

Does God exist in your lover?

Does God exist in you?

When you love your lover, are you sending your love to one single place?

What if you didn't direct your love to a *single* location?

What if you allowed the love to flow from you in all directions simultaneously?

What if you included all things in your love?

Does that diminish your love?

Being in love is your *natural state*.

As you include all things in this flow, your love multiplies beyond human comprehension.

Don't limit your love; expand it!

The Divine Matrix of Love

The most potent prayers begin with surrender.

When you surrender to the Divine, you align yourself with the most powerful energies in the universe.

Surrendering to the Divine means lovingly offering your energies to God, to be used as part of divine will.

"Thy will, not mine, be done."

When you surrender to the Divine, you allow God to work through you.

As you align your energies with universal love, you open yourself to changes beyond your current perceptions.

Universal love is so exceedingly powerful, yet so exceptionally gentle, that your job becomes simply *letting it work* in your life.

As you give yourself to the divine matrix of love, your prayers become more powerful because they are emanating from the source of all creation: Love.

A loving thought towards another becomes a divine blessing.

Time and space are nonexistent.

Illusions of separateness crumble.

All wishes become holy wishes.

Every thought becomes a prayer.

Surrender to the Divine and let love rule your life.

Is Your Life on Hold?

Are you waiting for something to happen in your life so that you can continue?

Have you put any aspect of your life "on hold?"

Become aware of how "waiting" feels.

Notice that the very thought of "waiting" puts a block in your energy flow.

Now think about what it feels like to remove this block and allow energy to freely flow through you.

Imagine *not waiting* anymore.

Think about doing or being whatever it is you've put on hold.

See it, feel it, hear it, taste it and smell it!

Allow every atom in your body to experience it.

Now, what are you waiting for?

Feel the blocks.

Are you ready to let them go?

What small steps can you take right now to release these blocks?

Begin now, one step at a time, building stepping stones to your goals.

Experience how good it feels *not to wait*.

Experience how good it feels to let go of the barriers and let you dreams manifest.

What are you waiting for now?

To Receive Comfort, Give Comfort

Everyone suffers loss.

Sometimes the loss is so great, it's as if your heart has been ripped out of your chest.

There seems to be no light in your life.

Your vision is dark.

Even tears offer no relief.

It's as though joy will never visit you again.

All you want to do is stop the pain.

All souls go through these horrible, dark times.

At these sad times, there are no consoling words.

Some turn to anger.

Some turn to hatred.

Some get stuck in the darkness of self-pity.

How could this happen?

Why did this happen?

What did I do wrong?

You cease living in the center of your being and grab at the fragments of energy that have been taken away.

This is when forgetting one's self, rising above the pain, and reaching out to help others becomes a path back to the light.

You receive comfort as you give it.

The brightness returns as you become a light in the lives of others.

Don't seek to escape your loss; seek to share it with others.

You must *become* the comforter to receive comfort.

Every Occurrence is to Your Advantage

One tiny perceptual shift can change your life.

Consider it a game.

What if you decide that every single thing that happens in your life is to your advantage?

Everything!

Even occurrences that appear negative are really designed to serve your highest good in some way.

Acknowledge that you don't know *how* your highest good is being met, but that it is.

Think of it!

A flat tire,

A terminal illness,

A relationship breakup,

The loss of a loved one,

Financial setbacks,

Weeds in your garden,

A bad hair day,

A pimple on the end of your nose!

Imagine how different your life would be if you looked at all these things as necessary for your personal evolution.

When you begin looking at things in this manner, your whole life will change.

You'll stop running from problems and start solving them.

Your enthusiasm will increase.

Your courage will be endless.

Your joy will have no limits.

Just one, tiny shift makes all the difference in the world—all the difference in *your* world!

Be Fearless – And Love!

To *be* loved *you* must love.

When someone *loves you*, who feels the love?

When *you love* someone, who feels the love?

Your heart breaks *not* when someone stops loving you, but when *you* stop loving.

You don't need to stop loving another for any reason whatsoever.

There is absolutely *no reason* to stop loving.

Loving doesn't mean you condone inappropriate behavior.

Loving another doesn't mean you accept abuse.

It doesn't mean you accept negative behavior.

You wouldn't love yourself if you accepted negativity, and all love starts with self-love.

Loving is accepting and embracing another on a deep, inner soul-level, regardless of whether that love is returned.

When you allow yourself the freedom to love, you become fearless.

As you become fearless, you become *free to love*.

The more you love, the more you evolve.

Your life is enriched.

You become stronger.

You become fearless.

Love, and be fearless!

෴ ෴ ෴

Be Anchored in Your Being

Rituals are designed to anchor you to a state of being.

A string of beads can anchor you to a prayerful state of mind.

A red traffic light can anchor you to a state of anger.

A time of day can anchor you to a state of meditation.

A smile, deeply felt, can anchor every cell in your body to a sense of well-being.

A lie can anchor you to a sense of guilt and mistrust.

Cigarettes and other habits can anchor you to some kind of deeply rooted emotional state that only the unconscious mind knows.

As you mature, it's important to know what your anchors are and to what states they are anchoring you.

As you become more aware, you can give up negative anchors and develop positive ones.

As you consciously develop anchors, you gain control of your energy.

Learning to use your energies appropriately is one of the main reasons you're here.

If you can't choose how you use the energies you have, what can you choose?

Anchors are like buttons that automatically control your energy.

Choosing your anchors and rituals allows you to choose your level of consciousness, your state of being and the quality of your life!

What rituals and anchors have you chosen?

Devotion

How often do you tell God you love Him?
How you honor God is important.
The important thing is to cultivate devotion.
God doesn't need your devotion, but *you* do.
You may think of God as Goddess, or the creative power of the universe, or simply your higher power, but it's important to let the love flow to this concept outside of yourself.

This flow allows a connection to be established.

The flow of love allows the veil of separation to vanish.

The flow of love allows you to become one with God and all others, since God *is in* all others.

When you allow love to flow, you are allowing yourself to be unified with the unlimited field of *all that is.*

Devotion to God enhances your life in ways you can't possibly imagine.

The flow of love allows you to have a mystical union with all that is holy.

Cultivate your own way of loving God.

Part of your uniqueness is your unique way of loving.

You can't do it wrong, so just do it!

How often do you tell God you love Him?

಄ ಄ ಄

The Mysteries of the Breath

Your breath is one of your body's most powerful tools.
Through it, you take in the force of life itself.

Your breath has the ability to purify, invigorate, and enlighten the body, mind, and spirit.

Without breath, the body ceases to function.

Most take the breath for granted, as one might take one's eyes and ears for granted.

Yet the breath is another avenue through which higher consciousness and union with the divine can be achieved.

You have the gifts you need to realize oneness.

It's simply a matter of which gifts suit you best.

Pay attention to your breath.

Honor it.

Learn its mysteries.

Become aware of your breath when you are frightened.

Become aware of your breath when you are angry.

Notice how it changes when your emotional state changes.

See if you can change your emotional state by changing the rhythm of your breath.

Your breath can be the focus through which your life changes.

Indeed, your breath is the vehicle through which you entered this life.

The mysteries of the breath are gateways into the mysteries of life.

ᕳᕲ ᕳᕲ ᕳᕲ

Prayers from the Heart

Your blessings and prayers are of extreme value.

One of the ways you develop your soul is through prayer.

Formal prayers are beneficial when you are first learning to send positive energy.

As you progress, it is important to allow the blessings to come from your heart.

Prayers from the heart are more powerful because they are more focused and uniquely express individuality.

They're like singing your own personal song to the universe.

Your personal song benefits every atom and molecule in the universe.

The harmony of your blessings extends beyond the farthest reaches you can imagine; balancing, soothing, and caressing.

You may think you are praying only for one person or one situation, but the benefits extend into eternity.

The value of your prayers extends forever.

Prayers are like gifts from the God-part of you.

The more you pray, the more you develop this God-part.

Praying from your heart is one of the most important uses of your energy.

Pray from your heart and the whole universe is blessed.

☙ ☙ ☙

You *Had* to be Created

God's love for you is greater than you can ever imagine.

This divine energy created not only you, but also the entire universe!

You are as important as each galaxy that exists in infinite space.

You are as great as a star!

God's love for you is so strong that you had to manifest!

And as great as God's love is for you, no one can love God in the exact same way you can!

Even though we are all composed of the same loving energy, each composition is different.

When you realize that the energy of God's love is what created you, you can tap into this inner force and use it as *your motivation* to create.

Once you begin using this love as your motivation, you truly begin developing in God's image.

That's where co-creation comes in.

God created you, and as you tap into this inner, divine energy and use it as your motivating source, you co-create with Him.

You become mother, father, child, and co-creator all in one.

The illusion of separation is gone.

Fear is over.

You have discovered your true nature: Love.

You had to be created to manifest your unique expression of love!

There is nothing greater than you in God's eyes!

Life Mastery

The ability to focus your attention is one of the most important skills you can master.

By harnessing this energy, you develop a force that will lead to life mastery.

What is "life mastery" other than control of your energies?

If you can't control your own energies, where is your power?

If you aren't controlling your power, who or what is?

One way to learn to focus is through meditation.

That's why the sages have touted meditation as a necessary practice for eons.

Meditation, by definition, is focusing your attention on a single object or idea.

That's the *first step* in life mastery and it requires *practice.*

Regardless of how long one has been meditating, whether it's one week or thirty years, it is still called "practice."

It's not that you don't get better at it, it's that you don't stop doing it.

It's like physical exercise.

To keep the benefits, you keep exercising.

Meditation is exercising the muscles of the mind.

You must master your attention before you master anything else.

Master your attention and you will master your life.

இ இ இ

The Truth About Your Limitations

The truth about your limitations is that they are here to *serve you*.

Your limitations are designed to force you into growth.

Your limitations, whatever they are - fear, hatred, jealousy, resentment, impatience - force you to do inner work if you want to release them.

Ask your particular vice what it wants for you.

What inner need is it trying to satisfy?

You may not be able to get meaningful answers if you do this work on a conscious, thinking level.

Go into a meditative state and ask the part of you that generated the limitation what it wants for you.

It ultimately wants you to experience a positive state, like peace, love or happiness.

Once you have discovered the gift behind this negativity, you can let it go, as it has served its purpose.

Thank the part of you that created this limitation.

Allow yourself to access the inner gift it wanted for you, and the negativity will be released.

When you discover the truth about your limitations, they will transform into gifts.

Cultivate Your Ideal Self and Manifest Miracles

Have you ever thought about how *you want to be*, at your very best?

Go deep inside now, and get in touch with that part of you that represents your ideal self.

Experience what it *feels like*, on all levels of your being, in every area of your life.

What does that inner picture look like, the picture of you, at your best?

Is it in color, or black and white?

Is it close to you, or far away?

Is it large, or is it small?

Is it bright, or is it dim?

Is it clear, or is it fuzzy?

What are you wearing and what is in the background?

Now, make this picture of you in full, brilliant color.

Bring it close to you and make it life-size.

Make it as bright and clear as you possibly can.

Now *step into the picture* of your ideal self.

As you step into your picture, take a deep breath.

Experience how good it feels to be you, the way you've always wanted to be, the person you came here to manifest!

Let this ideal be your guide in all future activities and decisions.

If you forget, take a deep breath to access your ideal.

If you have a decision to make, access your ideal and ask, "What would you do?"

It's natural to manifest miracles when you cultivate your ideal self.

౿ఌ ౿ఌ ౿ఌ

Your Life Depends on You!

What kind of person do you want to be?

Warm, kind, loving?

Vengeful, cruel, mean?

Forgiving, compassionate, helpful?

What precepts do you want to embrace?

"Trust in the Lord?"

Or, "An eye for an eye?"

Decide how you *want to be* and what qualities you want to exemplify.

You are only a slave to how you *have been* and what you *have believed* in the past if you *think* you are.

You have the ability to take your power back from previous conditioning and use it in the present moment to create who you want to be *now*.

Allow yourself to become deeply aware of what it feels like to be your *ideal self*.

Feel the positive emotions as you access these qualities.

Notice that these qualities are within you *now*, at this very moment.

Experience how good it feels to breathe in these positive traits, and let them permeate all levels of your being.

Become aware of how wonderful it feels to access the parts of you that *represent you*, at your very best.

Focus on bringing these parts to the surface.

Energize these qualities with your attention and you'll naturally create your ideal self.

Your life depends on *you!*

Allow Your Holy Life to Burst Forth!

There is a divine nature within you waiting to burst forth!

This divine nature is so holy and powerful that you may have trouble recognizing it as part of you.

You may have been taught that you need to be humble.

You may have been taught that you are unholy.

You may believe that you are a bad person who must learn how to be good.

What will help you have a leap in evolution is the realization that what you have inside of you, underneath the self-imposed negativity, shines so brightly with holiness that it's, at first, overwhelming.

Scriptures from all the great holy traditions teach to go within.

There are clues written throughout history.

Many sacred writings have described holy quests.

It is up to you to make this divine journey, and it doesn't require "going" anywhere.

It requires becoming aware of what is holy *within you.*

This awareness results from the *inner* journey.

"Seek and ye shall find."

"The kingdom of heaven is within."

Begin to love the God in you.

Discover the God within and allow your holy life to burst forth!

When Life Comes Crashing In

Sometimes life comes crashing in on top of you with devastation.

You may feel the weight of responsibility and tragedy.

You may feel defeated and powerless.

You may feel you have failed and will never succeed.

Your job is to recognize that these times are to be faced and handled with poise.

Spiritual evolvement doesn't mean life gets easier.

As you evolve, you are able to handle even more difficult circumstances, precisely because of your evolvement.

Don't think that because something difficult happens, you've done something wrong to create it.

Think instead of the best way you can rise above it.

Change being a victim into being victorious.

Everyone is given the inner resources to handle whatever life throws at them.

When life comes crashing in, ask yourself what you can do to remedy the situation.

Your role may be to set an example.

Your role may be to teach.

Experience life not as if you've done something wrong, but as if you've done something *right*.

Ask what you can learn and what you can teach others.

When life comes crashing in, turn devastation into evolution.

∽ ∽ ∽

Selfish Love is an Oxymoron

Love of self is not selfish.

Self-love and self-absorption are opposites.

Honest, pure love of self is a requirement for evolution.

Love is the most powerful force in the universe.

Think of love as wondrous, awestruck attention.

At first, most people require an external object upon which to focus love.

This can be a lover, a guru, an idea, a baby…any number of things.

These external objects, however, are *designed* to fail you.

They *must fail* so that you are forced to turn inward.

Once you have developed self-love, you have unconditional love to shower on all external things.

Once you have developed internal love, the veil of separation lifts and you realize *all is one*.

This realization allows you to love in a whole new way.

This discovery of universal truth is a leap in awareness from which you can never return.

Nor would you want to.

When you discover the God in you, you automatically discover the God in others.

Others will never fail you after this, because you don't put your trust in *them*.

You put your trust in *God*.

You put your trust in the God within you.

Learn to love the God within yourself and you will learn to love the God within all.

Nurture with Nature

If at all possible, spend time outside, alone with nature.

Simply being with nature, with no distractions, has wonderful effects on the body, mind, and spirit.

Become aware of how plants grow.

Notice the texture of the soil.

Feel the air on your skin.

Smell the fragrances of each different plant.

Experience the joy of an opening flower.

Feel the sun's energy penetrating your bones.

Become aware of how the animals live completely *in the present moment*.

If possible, stand or sit directly on the earth and let your energies meld.

Feel the earth's strength entering your body, filling you with its energy.

Thank the planet for providing you with such an awesome, wondrous place to live!

Feel the earth's loving essence circulate throughout your entire being.

Become aware of the splendor of each growing thing.

Experience the joy the earth exudes into all aspects of itself.

Each atom – so precious!

Each thought – so magnificent!

And *you* are a part of it, *now and forever!*

It's called nature (nurture) for a reason.

෨ ෨ ෨

Connecting to God

When you talk to God, every word is heard.

God hears not only every word you say, but also every hidden meaning, and every hidden *intention* behind them.

When you speak to God, you open a magical doorway of communication.

The answers you receive through this doorway echo through the universe until they reach your ears.

As you begin this connection to God, your life will change in more wondrous ways than you can imagine.

As you begin this journey with God, you begin to live in two different worlds, heaven and earth, at the same time!

Heaven becomes brighter, earth becomes clearer, and your perceptions become deeper.

Don't ever think that God doesn't hear you or that He doesn't respond.

When you think you don't get an answer, ask yourself, "Am I being still enough to listen?"

Practice being still and you will hear God's answers echoing throughout the universe.

God always answers.

It's up to you to learn to listen.

You Have No Limits!

There is no end to growing, becoming, and discovering.
You exist as part of an unlimited, infinite hologram.
There is no end to this multi-dimensional field.

The more you explore and learn about yourself, the more you understand the world.

This world has unlimited dimensions and unlimited planes.
You don't *create* this world; you *are* this world!

This world exists inside of you and outside of you simultaneously.

"As above, so below."

As you mature spiritually, you discover these worlds, these dimensions, and these planes *inside* of you.

At the same time, you become aware of them *outside* of you.

Because you live in unlimited realms, you have access to unlimited skills, wisdom, and love.

You take a leap in spiritual maturity when you realize that there are *no limits!*

When you access this infinite hologram, you transcend your physical boundaries and overcome any limitations you believed you had.

What is on the other side of the unlimited field?
What is on the other side of God?
There is no other side because the infinite field, God, has no limits.

You are in this field now; growing, becoming, and discovering, without end.

There is no end to this field and there is *no end to you!*

∾ ∾ ∾

Seeing Through the Eyes of Love

There may be times of emptiness.

There may be times you feel alone or ill.

Know that these times are *temporary* and will pass.

Seek to learn the good that will come out of such experiences.

Always lift yourself up to *find the positive* in all situations, even if you have to search to discover the good.

As long as you focus on what is good and kind and loving, you will grow.

You will not only grow, you will *flourish*.

Stagnation occurs when you get stuck in negativity.

Focus on the good and you will see the situation, the emptiness, the illness, from a higher level.

This higher level is a portal through which a perceptual shift can occur.

Once this occurs, all things are seen in a different light: The light of love.

When you look at anything through the eyes of love, you automatically see the good.

When you see through the eyes of love, you allow the God in you to grow.

The veil of illusion lifts.

There is no emptiness, no isolation, no illness.

All is one; perfect, pure, and whole.

Illness is temporary and easier to endure when you know your true self is one with the Divine.

Let it be easier.

Love yourself.

Look for the good and you will see through the eyes of love.

The Magic of Stillness

You may be afraid to be still, afraid to be quiet, because of what you *think* you'll discover about yourself.

If so, you have mistakenly identified with your negativities. What you must remember is that *you are not* your foibles. You are *not* your character defects.

Those are the first things you notice as you become still, because they are closest to the surface.

As you go deeper, you discover that underneath is something so positive and beautiful and bright that it's almost overwhelming.

The enormity, the magnificence of what lies at your very core is fabulous beyond your wildest imagination!

The knowledge of this reality is life changing.

That's why the yogis and the mystics spend so much of their time alone in meditation, to get a glimpse of their souls.

The same thing that exists in them exists in you.

The same thing that exists in you exists in them.

The only difference is that they know it and you don't.

They have acknowledged their inner adversaries.

They know that everyone has negative aspects.

They simply give themselves permission to go deeper into themselves until they discover the magic of stillness.

Don't be afraid of what's inside you.

The transforming power of stillness can take you to pure bliss.

∾ ∾ ∾

Falling in Love

Do you want to know the secret to attracting your dream lover?

It's simple: Fall in love with *yourself first!*

When you fall in love with yourself, you allow an energy to develop that is magnetic.

This energy is not arrogance or self-absorption.

It is a true realization of the God within.

It is cultivating a deep respect for the holiness that exists at the center of your being.

This is *true love*.

As you develop true love for yourself, it radiates to others.

You attract those who have energy that is complimentary to yours.

If you go deep inside and make decisions from this place of love, you will remain true to yourself and avoid the pitfalls of co-dependency when you enter in to a relationship.

Co-dependence comes from neediness, not love.

When you truly love yourself, there is no neediness, no emptiness.

Love has no beginning, no middle, and no end.

Love is forever and exists within you at this very moment.

Tap into this endless inner flow of energy and begin loving yourself so that others can too!

◌ ◌ ◌

Experiencing Miracles

There may be times when you find yourself in circumstances over which you have no control.

These are the times when it is imperative that you focus on the good.

Always focus on the highest possible good in any given situation.

There is something good to be found in all things.

Put your attention on that positive aspect and watch the goodness grow.

Positive energy *creates*.

Negative energy *destroys*.

If you want healing, abundance, uplifting of any kind, focus your attention on something positive.

If you are in physical pain, remember that you are in your body *temporarily*, and put your attention on something outside of your body, like a flower or a soothing piece of music.

When you find yourself experiencing any negativity, go to an inner place of tranquility, so that the body can regenerate.

Any kind of nervousness, anxiety, upset, fear, anger, resentment, remorse or guilt is degenerative.

Learn to catch your thinking when it is involved in these negative aspects; focus on something positive instead.

Regardless of how small that positive aspect is at first, put your attention on it and watch the goodness grow.

You may not always have control over external circumstances, but you can gain control over internal ones.

If you want to experience miracles, *think miracles!*

෨ ෨ ෨

The Value of Mistakes

Following your heart may not be easy.

Sometimes you don't know what you want or the best thing to do.

Many times choices are not clear.

You may feel like you're groping through thick fog.

Sometimes there are no "right" choices.

How do you judge "right" anyway?

You have to be willing to make mistakes or you become paralyzed.

What is a "mistake?"

A mistake is something that you would not choose to do again, but you may only know this in retrospect.

Not knowing what to do is one of the major causes of stress.

Living with uncertainty becomes debilitating.

You seek awareness of "right" action.

Sometimes, however, you must sit in "not knowing."

Remember to ask your angels and your guides to help you.

Remember that you are not alone.

Accept inner guidance, no matter how subtle it is.

Accepting inner guidance will help you become in tune with your heart.

Part of your job here is to make mistakes.

Making mistakes is akin to putting up guideposts along your path.

You learn what direction to go and where *not* to turn.

Your mistakes help create your spiritual map.

That's why mistakes have value!

Internal Paradise

Joy and tranquility exist in this very instant.

Hatred and hostility also exist in this very instant.

What is the difference between experiencing extremes?

The difference is a decision you make, moment-by-moment, to experience either peace and tranquility, or hatred and hostility.

Do you realize the power you have to make such life-changing choices?

At this very instant you have the power to *choose* what you feel!

You have the power to create your internal experience, regardless of what's going on outside of you!

Regardless of your past, present, or future, you have the power to create an internal paradise.

The interesting thing to notice about this internal paradise is that the stronger you make it on the inside, the easier it is to manifest on the outside.

You are not creating a fantasy world!

You are empowering yourself by making honest, clear choices about how you are directing your energies in this moment.

Choose to be still.

Listen to divine stillness.

Tap into positive, loving energies and create paradise!

ᗏ ᗏ ᗏ

Make Friends With Your Fear

Until you look at your worst fear, your deepest secret, your greatest regret – square in the eye – it's going to control you.

It may control you in subtle ways, like creating a sense of unease or mild anxiety.

It may control you in more obvious ways, like the need to overeat, smoke cigarettes, drink alcohol or use other mind-altering drugs.

The irony is that this secret, this fear, really wants you to feel good, it just doesn't know how to get you there.

This part of you is probably very young, maybe even an infant, that's why it has no mature coping skills.

Make friends with this part of you.

Instead of running away through distractions, face it, embrace it, tell it that you love it, thank it, and ask what it *really wants* for you.

Keep asking until you get to a state of being that is positive and complete within itself, like happiness or bliss.

Allow yourself to feel this completely.

Make it strong!

Let this fabulous state permeate every atom of your being.

Practice accessing this positive state.

You are the only one who can experience how good it feels, just as you are the only one who felt the fear, or kept the secret, or had the regret.

Make friends with your fear and find out what positive state it wants for you.

∿ ∿ ∿

You Are a Holy Master

Once you realize how important you are to the universe, your doubts will vanish.

You are a holy master in development.

The very *process* of your development is holy.

Who you are and who I am are exactly the same, yet different.

You have many of the same thoughts, emotions, desires, needs, and wants as I do.

Your job on this planet is just as important as mine.

We are basically the same, and yet miraculously different.

These differences are to be honored, cherished, and loved.

Each flower, each star, is vitally important, just as you are.

Each particle of the universe resonates to each of your thoughts, regardless of how insignificant you think they are.

The vibration of your existence is felt beyond the farthest reaches of the universe.

The power of who you are cannot be exaggerated.

You not only *make* a difference; you *are* a difference!

What kind of difference are you?

What kind of difference are you becoming?

When you stop doubting your importance, your growth naturally accelerates.

Embrace your holiness.

Help the universe grow!

◌ ◌ ◌

Is Flower Power Literal?

Just as rain from the heavens cleans the planet's atmosphere, the natural forces of nature can cleanse your personal energies.

Nature's organic energies help clear your thinking and purify your heart.

That's one reason confusion runs rampant in urban areas.

Your body, mind, and spirit crave the nourishment you receive from water, rocks, plants, and animals.

The term "flower power" can be more literal than metaphorical.

Flowers have the power to soothe, strengthen, and sweeten.

What magnificent powers these are!

Focus on the beauty of one drop of water glistening on a rose petal.

There is an entire universe in that drop of water!

And there is an entire universe inside of you, unfolding as you grow.

Nature *wants* to serve you.

The energies in nature delight in your requests for comfort.

As you connect with the natural, universal forces, you avail yourself of their healing, loving energies.

Join your forces with nature and see what happens.

Oneness with All

What do you honor and love?

To what are you devoted?

These are ways of asking: What helps your energies become loving?

Cultivating loving energies is one of the most important activities in which you can engage.

As you cultivate loving energies, your entire energetic field expands.

The more you love, the greater capacity you develop *to* love.

Notice how your body feels different as you allow yourself to experience love.

Notice how your thinking changes.

You actually see things differently.

Find one thing outside of yourself to honor.

It can be anything you value.

It can be a plant, a cloud, a person, or an idea.

Let this honor grow into devotion.

Let the devotion expand.

Notice how your perception changes.

Now find one thing *inside* yourself to honor.

It can be any quality you appreciate.

Let that appreciation grow into devotion.

Let that devotion expand until there is no separation between what you love *outside* yourself and what you love *inside* yourself.

As you practice this technique, the illusion of separation lifts and your oneness with all is revealed.

What you love and honor on the inside merges with the outside and *becomes* your life!

Holy Communion

When you are going on a journey, send your angels out before you to prepare the way.

Send your angels to meet others' angels and establish a connection.

Ask your angels to discuss any specific issues, on either side, that need addressing.

If you do this beforehand, you are allowing work to be done on the spiritual plane that would take hours, days, or years to accomplish on the physical plane.

Your angels can soften the hearts and prepare the minds of people with whom you have contact.

Your job is then to trust that everything that could be done has been done.

Trust that whatever happens is serving everyone's highest good.

This request also helps *you* have a pure heart and clear mind.

It allows both your higher self and those of others to merge.

This action establishes holy communication.

Holy communication (Holy Communion) establishes the path to spiritual evolution.

You are the giver, as well as the receiver, of this holy union.

Think of every encounter you have with another as an opportunity for Holy Communion.

Ask your angels to help.

Communicating with your angels is also a Holy Communion!

Dreams are the Gateway to the Universe

Where do you "go" each night when you "go to sleep?"
Dreams are more than a fantasy.

Dreams can be the gateway through which communication with other realms is possible.

Dreams can hold the key to the past, the present, and the future.

When you dream, you are accessing that level of consciousness through which you communicate with your angels and spirit guides.

You are also accessing the state of consciousness through which communication with those who have crossed over to the other side is possible.

In the dream state, you have access to the unlimited field of wisdom and understanding.

One requirement necessary to utilize this information is that you must remember it.

Another skill required of a dream master is to be *conscious* of the dreams.

Ask your higher self and your angels to assist you in remembering your dreams, and soon you will develop this skill.

Ask every night before you go to sleep.

Then record your dreams upon awakening.

Either write them down or speak into a recorder.

Soon you will be able to ask for information regarding any conceivable subject.

You will not only "go to sleep," but you will *remember* where you've gone and what you've learned!

If all you're doing is sleeping at night, you're wasting a lot of precious time.

Angel Multiplication

You may experience fear or a lack of self-confidence because you feel you have to accomplish tasks alone.

Perhaps you forgot that you have legions of angels waiting for you to ask for their help.

Most times they help without asking, but when you do call on them, their energy is multiplied specifically for your use.

Your angels delight in assisting you.

You can ask for guidance not only in physical ways, such as ensuring a safe trip, but also in emotional ways, such as letting go of resentment or anger.

You can ask for help in forgiveness, in learning how to love, or in being a better example.

There is nothing too mundane for your angels' help.

There are "special interest" angels whose sole purpose is to help you with specific tasks.

Your job is to make your requests honestly and sincerely, without frivolity.

When you ask earnestly, your angels are eager to help.

When you *know* you are not alone, no matter what you're doing, you have no need to be afraid.

You have all the help you need, just ask!

Dealing with Depression

Dealing with depression is easier if you dissociate from your own thoughts.

Depression begins when you start taking your negative thoughts seriously.

The first step is to become aware of that *first* negative thought.

As you become aware of that thought, realize that *you are not* that thought.

That thought is simply an electrical impulse that has traveled through your brain, and has absolutely *no power* over you.

You do not have to act on that thought.

When that thought pops into your mind, simply observe it in the same manner you would observe a set of car keys or a pair of shoes.

Do the car keys or the shoes have power over you?

Of course not!

Neither does that negative thought.

Now replace that negative thought with two positive thoughts.

Anything that is pleasant and enjoyable will do.

Keep up this practice, and soon your depressing thoughts will cease to be bothersome.

You will learn to recognize them for what they are – depressing thoughts – *not you!*

Thoughts only have the power you give them.

Give your power to positive thoughts and negative thoughts don't have a chance!

Letting God Work Through You

Go deep inside yourself and connect with an inner point of peace.

Let this point of peace glow and expand until its light fills your entire being.

Experience how good it feels to allow this light of peace fill every cell in your body.

Now, from this vantage point, become aware of a situation that concerns you.

Notice how much easier it is to see solutions from this perspective of peace.

If the situation with which you are concerned seems overwhelming, allow the luminescence to grow and encompass it.

Envelop this situation with the light of calmness, peace, and trust.

This inner place of trust and love is where *God works through you*.

From this place, problems are seen through the light of clarity and love.

Solutions present themselves as if by magic.

There is no struggle, no strife, as all things become blessed.

The more you visit this place of inner peace, the more the light can grow.

Your job is to go within to this place of peace, so that God *can* work through you!

Sending Love Allows it to Return

Many times when you feel a lack of self-confidence, it is because you think someone has withdrawn love from you.

It may be a friend, a lover, a parent, or a spouse.

One way to deal with this is to send that person love.

Visualize that person in your mind's eye and surround him or her with the sparkling white light of God's love.

If you have trouble visualizing, that's okay.

Simply allow the love to flow from your heart to theirs.

Allow your love to fill their heart until it overflows, surrounding them in an aura of energy, like a bubble.

Know *now* that what *they think* has *nothing* to do with *you!*

What *you think* has *everything* to do with *you!*

What *you think* about *that person* has everything to do with what you *feel* about *yourself.*

That's why it's so important to send *only love to others.*

Who feels the love you send to others?

Send the love right now.

Notice *now* what has happened to your level of self-confidence.

The only one who can withdraw love is *you!*

As you allow love to flow from you, it returns, and you are naturally confident.

Manifesting Magically

When all of your energetic systems are in alignment, your goals will manifest as if by magic.

The effort is not so much *making* things happen on the outside as it is getting things to *agree* on the inside.

Once your heart, mind, and body agree on something, it is actually quite easy for it to manifest.

It's getting all the inner systems working together that require discipline and practice.

Begin with a simple task.

Think about accomplishing this task.

Are there any conflicting thoughts?

What are they?

Experience how it would feel if you had *already completed* the task.

How does it feel?

Move one small step toward this goal.

Is there any resistance?

From which system, the heart, mind or body, is this resistance coming?

Learn to identify the system so you can address the difficulty.

What does the difficulty want?

What is the difficulty trying to say?

Let it speak to you, either in words, feelings, or pictures and identify its purpose.

As each purpose is satisfied, the energy flows freely and alignment is achieved.

Once alignment is achieved, see how easily your goals become reality.

It happens as if *by magic!*

Death is Not a Disaster

The body is not designed to last indefinitely.

The body is a vehicle through which you, the soul, are allowed to live in this realm.

Living in this realm provides the opportunity for you to learn and develop in ways that would otherwise be difficult.

To mature in this realm requires patience, tolerance, compassion, forgiveness, and love.

These are characteristics you can more easily develop here because of the temporal nature of existence.

If "death" didn't exist here, there would be no need to develop forgiveness.

You could literally hold a grudge forever, because there would be no need to change.

Because of this realm's nature, you have the opportunity to advance your soul by "taking a break" after you leave your body.

If you stayed in this realm forever, it would be extremely difficult to experience such a drastic perceptual shift.

Death allows you to rest, to recuperate from the pains of this world.

It reunites you with your soul group and helps you gain insights from an entirely different point of view.

Death is not a disaster.

Death is an opportunity for assessment, rejuvenation, and exploration.

Don't Lash Out, Love!

When your feelings have been hurt, there is a tendency to lash out in return.

You may think if you injure the one who offended you, your own pain will diminish.

It's a preposterous thought, but one believed by many.

Hurting another in return only distracts you momentarily from your own pain.

It's a way of putting the pain outside so you don't have to feel it.

Of course, it doesn't work.

Temporary distraction only delays your personal growth.

What you need to do to heal the pain is recognize that it's there in the first place.

As you become aware, you can ask yourself: Why it is so painful?

What part of you has been injured?

Your pride?

Your ego?

Your self-image?

Are you angry with yourself for reacting with deep emotion?

Do you need to forgive the person who hurt you?

Do you need to forgive yourself?

As you learn to *respond with love* instead of anger, you realize there is nothing to forgive, as you have *not passed judgment* in the first place!

Respond with love and you will recover from being hurt much more quickly.

Don't lash out, *love!*

❧ ❧ ❧

The Holy Spirit Within All

All plants, animals, people, and minerals have a blueprint for their ideal expression of consciousness.

This holy consciousness represents the ideal on all levels, both physical and metaphysical.

Your development is enhanced as you tap into this holy consciousness.

As you access the blueprint for your creation, it becomes easier to manifest.

Many have never considered their ideal self.

You may not have given thought to your own representation of excellence.

Yet you have the blueprint of perfection within.

As you go into meditation and ask to be shown this holy blueprint, it is revealed.

The more you become aware of its existence, the easier it is to create.

As you put your attention on your ideal self, you give it energy.

The energy of attention helps it to manifest in the physical world.

Go within.

Get in touch with your ideal self and allow it to emerge.

ᘯ ᘯ ᘯ

Surrender to the Divine

As you invite God into your life, be prepared for miracles.

Accept the revelation that divine energy is working in your life in wondrous ways.

It may not always *seem* as if the miraculous is unfolding in your life.

Work through times of doubt by simply trusting *even more*.

The instant a problem pops into your mind, remember to give it to God.

Divine energy has the ability to transform your problems in ways that are beyond your understanding.

This where trust comes in.

As you surrender to the Divine, begin to see everything in your life as if God orchestrated it.

See all the people in your life as if they serve a specific, divine purpose.

Begin to see the *positive intentions* behind all of your difficulties.

Begin to see your problems as opportunities for you to develop heavenly characteristics.

Invite God in your life and watch the joy of surrender unfold.

Discover Your Life's Purpose

Do you know why you are on this planet?

Do you know what you came here to learn?

When you know your purpose, it becomes the focal point of the fabulous mosaic that is your life.

Knowing why you are here helps makes sense out of chaos.

There is a part of you that knows your life's purpose.

This part is the higher self.

To become aware of what the higher self knows, it is important for the connection between your conscious self and your higher self to become stronger.

Go deep inside and ask your higher self to give you a symbol that will remind you that the connection has been strengthened.

Ask your higher self why you are here?

What did you come here to learn?

Your life's purpose is usually simple, yet profound.

You may have come here to learn to love, to be of service, to overcome fear, to learn wisdom.

One lesson is not better than another; we each have to learn all lessons.

Go deep inside the stillness.

Allow your higher self to reveal your life's purpose.

Observe the beauty of your life's mosaic!

The Difference Between Pain and Suffering

If you are experiencing physical, emotional or mental pain, know that it is *temporary*.

Know that it is possible to experience pain *without* suffering.

Suffering is what you feel when you *involve yourself* in the state of pain.

Most humans will experience pain of one kind or another throughout life.

You can diminish and shorten these times by removing your attachment to them.

When you put your attention on the pain, you give it energy.

Become aware of the pain, and then redirect your attention.

This is not the same as denial.

Denial is pretending the pain doesn't exist in the first place.

To experience pain without suffering, you must first acknowledge it and what is causing it.

This allows you to work through the healing process without identifying with it.

When you identify with the pain, you suffer.

You are *not* the pain!

Who you *really are* is permanent and incapable of *suffering*.

When you identify with who you *really are*, you won't suffer, regardless of the pain.

Manifesting Spirit in the Physical Realms

It is essential to live *through* the physical body.

The insights, inspirations, and revelations you receive in the spiritual realms become valuable when you manifest them in the physical realms.

Part of the reason you are here is to bring the spiritual *into the physical*.

When the desire to create develops within you and you don't follow through, that energy can turn into frustration, anger, or resentment.

You unconsciously direct these negative emotions at yourself for not doing what you desire.

You become angry and frustrated with yourself.

Infinity works both ways.

"As above, so below."

The spiral of life flows *both ways*.

Developing a spiritual life that doesn't manifest in the physical life defeats the purpose of existence on this plane.

That's why manifesting your heart's desire is crucial.

It's in the process of manifestation that your life unfolds and your soul develops.

What is in your heart?

What are you manifesting in your life?

What are you creating through the use of your physical body?

Salvation Through Joy

It is your *duty* to experience joy.

Many have been taught that the path to God is paved with suffering.

Suffering has been glorified into an art form.

Martyrs are held in high esteem, and we are taught to emulate them.

Therefore, the more you suffer, the better you are.

You may think that the more miserable you are in this realm, the more "rewards" you'll receive in the next realm.

In truth, the more you suffer in this realm, the more you suffer, period.

The only virtue in suffering is realizing that you don't need to suffer.

Regardless of your circumstances, regardless of what has happened to you, your salvation depends on your ability to find joy.

When you experience the radiance of bliss, your vibrations are lifted and you are able to perceive even greater happiness.

You are able to share this happiness as you achieve it.

As joy is cultivated, you connect with God on an entirely new level.

To deny the *joy* of loving God is to deny God!

Do you think God wants you to suffer?

Suffering results when you *prevent* yourself from experiencing the joy of loving God.

Cultivate this joy, and experience the bliss of loving *all things*.

It's Not Personal

There may be times when you experience disappointment.
There may be times when your expectations are not met.
Family, friends or lovers may fail you.

It will be easier to get through these times if you remember that others' perceived "failings" have *nothing* to do with *you*.

It is *not personal*.

Others' actions are the result of *their needs* to fulfill their roles and destinies on this plane.

What they do has nothing to do with you personally.

Even if a lover betrays you, it is not personal.

That lover would have betrayed anyone in your position.

Your job is to learn and grow through each circumstance and experience, no matter how difficult.

Feel the disappointment.

Accept the betrayal.

Feel the angst in all its depth.

And then, give it to God.

Don't try to hide from the grief, but don't wallow in it either.

Allow yourself to experience the lesson so you can let the ache go.

Don't get stuck.

When you take it personally, you are staying stuck; you are not giving it to God.

It's impossible to avoid pain, but you can get through it more quickly when you realize that it's not personal.

∽ ∽ ∽

Sorrow's Remedy

Regardless of how "right" things are in your life, there will be times of sadness.

Sorrow is a natural human experience.

Don't try to resist sorrow or pretend it's not there.

Sadness must be honored, just as joy is honored.

We all experience difficult times.

The key word is "time."

The very nature of time is that it passes.

Time is *temporary.*

Sadness and physical pain are similar in that they exist in the linear, relative realm: The realm of time.

Sadness and pain can't be avoided and can't be denied.

You can get "through" these feelings more quickly, however, by rising above the earthly realm of consciousness and allowing yourself to perceive through a higher level of awareness.

This higher level of awareness is achieved through *allowing yourself to love* in spite of the sorrow.

Love helps lift you to a higher plane so you don't experience sadness the same way.

Allowing yourself to love is the only remedy for sorrow.

Don't deny sorrow – practice love.

᠙ ᠙ ᠙

The Currency of Time is Love

As you achieve stillness, the importance of each moment becomes crucial.

Every moment that is not *held in love* is a moment *wasted*.

Every thought that is not surrounded in love is a thought wasted.

When you think about how you are investing your time, what that really means is how you are investing your *love*.

When you think of time, think of "spending" time.

The currency of time is love.

When you realize that true abundance is true love, and that *you have the ability to allow true love to flow through you*, then you will also realize that your greatest accomplishment is to honor each moment, each thought, each person, with this unending love.

As you extend this love to all things, it comes back to you a thousandfold.

Imagine a love so powerful that it can turn darkness into light!

Imagine a love so powerful that it can turn hatred into peace; turmoil into calm; sickness into health; fear into forgiveness.

This is the power you have in each moment.

How are you spending *your* time?

❧   ❧   ❧

Your Greatest Power

There are things you can control and things you cannot.

You can save yourself much grief and suffering if you learn the difference early in life.

Can you determine if it's going to rain today?

No, but you can seek shelter if it does rain.

One of the greatest powers you can develop is the power to *choose your thoughts*.

Regardless of external circumstances, regardless of what is happening "to you," you have the power to choose *how to think* about these happenings.

You have the power to change your beliefs.

If you don't *believe* you have the power to change your thoughts, then you don't!

If you don't believe you have the ability to seek shelter from the rain, then you won't!

As you train your thinking, your personal power grows.

Begin controlling *how* you direct your thoughts.

Notice that by changing your thoughts, you can change the way you *feel*.

Notice that the more you choose your thoughts and the resulting feelings, the more control you have!

Experiment!

Your greatest power begins with your greatest thought!

Honor Your Work

It is an honor to work.

You may forget it is an honor because you may not be doing the kind of work that is your heart's desire.

Perhaps you don't know what your heart's desire is.

Think for a moment about what you would do if you could spend your time exactly the way you wanted.

What would you do?

Don't consider anything too outrageous!

Perhaps you would spend your time bobbing like a cork upon the ocean.

Perhaps you would be skiing on the snowy slopes of a gentle mountain.

Perhaps you would be reading a fabulously entertaining book.

Maybe you'd direct a movie, or write a play.

Maybe you'd be surfing a big wave or shaving points off your golf score.

Now consider continuing this activity eight hours a day, at least five days a week.

Is that how you really want to spend that much time?

Now think about the "work" you do.

Think about how that work is enhanced by also having the time to spend indulging in your heart's desire.

What is work and what is your heart's desire?

Become clear on this and your work will become easier.

Become clear on this and you will know it is an honor to work.

෨ ෨ ෨

The Ultimate Exercise of Using Free Will

How you think affects who you are.

One of your most important jobs is to determine *how* to use your thought-energy.

Don't worry about what thoughts pop into your mind.

(Worry is a form of thought-energy, isn't it?)

You may not have control over what pops into your mind, but you do have control over what you do with the thoughts once they are there.

The thoughts are not initially of value.

Horrible, hideous, grotesque thoughts may pop into your mind.

Those thoughts have no value except for you to learn to turn away from them.

Your assignment is to learn which thoughts to focus on and which thoughts to dismiss.

It's simply a matter of saying no to negative thought-energies, and yes to positive thought-energies.

As you say no to the negative ones, they diminish.

As you say yes to the positive ones, they increase.

This is the *ultimate exercise of free will*, exercising the ability to *choose your thoughts*.

Who would you *like to be?*

How do you imagine this person thinks?

Use your energies to think these thoughts!

Thought-energies have great power.

How you use this power determines *who you are.*

What are you thinking now?

Perfect Relationships

When you're not happy with a relationship, it's usually because you're not getting what you want.

That "want" is actually something in *your* life that is lacking.

You want it from another because you don't know how to give it to yourself.

The lesson of relationships is to give with no expectations.

True giving is not suffering, martyrdom, or sacrifice.

True giving is simply being the real you with whomever you're with.

Giving doesn't mean "giving up" something.

Giving means being free to express who you are.

When you freely give, you naturally receive nourishing energy because you are not coming from a place of "want."

As you develop the wholeness within, the need for approval from without diminishes.

Then you can truly love.

You can let the love flow unconditionally because it's not dependent on another's approval.

The relationship is no longer an issue because you are doing all you are supposed to do: *Love!*

When you love, there is no want.

When you *love yourself,* you are being the highest expression of who you are.

You are in perfect relationship with yourself!

༄ ༄ ༄

The Sound of Yourself

Listen to life!
Go outside and touch the earth.
Smell the air.
Taste the tartness of a three-leaf clover.
Feel the velvet of a rose petal.
Reconnect with the universe as you ground your senses in the planet.

Feel the firmness of your place on the earth and expand your consciousness into the heavenly realms simultaneously.

Appreciating the concrete reality of the earth helps to enhance the appreciation of the ethereal reality of higher consciousness.

That's why it's so important to quiet the mind.

Internal chatter distracts from the sounds of life.

As your attention becomes focused, your perception magnifies.

As your perception magnifies, you become more aware of the subtle realities.

Listen!

In the stillness you discover within, if you're quiet enough, you'll hear the sound of yourself.

That's the sound you were given ears to hear.

What is the sound of you?

What song in life were you given to play?

Each Magic Moment

Every moment has its magic.

The more you allow your consciousness to expand, the more you become aware of this magic.

It is the glory of the Holy Spirit working in the earthly realm that creates it.

This glory can be seen in the way a crystal reflects the light of sunshine.

It can be felt in the warm caress of moisture in the air.

It can be heard in the loud screech of a blue jay.

It can be tasted in the crunch of an apple.

It can be smelled in the dampness of the earth.

Most importantly, it can be perceived in the softness of your own heart, as you invite the Holy Spirit to work through you, caressing, hearing, and loving those around you, *through you!*

As you become a channel of love, the magic, the mystery, and the motion of life move through you in mystical ways.

You begin to see the holiness vibrating through each atom.

This "common" energy isn't common at all!

This energy that exists in all things is beyond the conception of holy!

It can't be created or destroyed.

It has no beginning, no middle, and no end!

It exists within and without all things!

It is ever changing, evolving – and yet it's the same!

It exists in each moment.

Discover the glory each day offers and honor the magic in each moment.

Your Place is Safe

Your particular place in this universe is guaranteed.

The energy that is you is safe.

Fear pulls you out of your center of energy, which is why fear is so debilitating.

As you become aware of how secure you are in your own energetic field, fear will have less influence over you.

Fear only has power in your life because you accept it as real.

You honor fear and validate it, thereby giving your power to an illusion!

The illusion grows and feeds on itself until it seems to exist independently of you.

How is this possible?

Where does fear exist if it doesn't exist *inside you?*

If fear exists independently of you, then that means there is some place in this universe that is not holy.

Where could such a place be?

Is there a place that exists *without God?*

Where is the fear when it is not within you?

Fear only exists because you give it your energy.

There is no room for fear when you fill all of your space with love.

What do you want to exist in *your space?*

Fill yourself with love and fear will vanish.

That's the magic of love!

Fill your place in the universe with love and your place is always safe!

You Are a Magnet for God's Grace

God's grace is always present.

It's simply up to you to receive it.

You become a better receiver as you become more joyful and accepting in your everyday life.

As you become more accepting of others, you become more accepting of God's grace.

As you clear yourself of the debris of resentment, anger, fear, and frustration, you free your energy channels to accept grace.

As you become clear, you become a magnet for God's grace.

What has been there all along is now attracted to you.

Your ability to be a channel of grace is only limited by your ability to accept it.

God doesn't limit grace.

There is no rationing of divine grace.

There are *no limits* to your ability to channel this grace.

The only limits you have are the limits you *think* you have.

That's why it is important to go to the place of *no thinking*, to the place of stillness, so divine grace can enter.

God's grace enters through the opening of your inner stillness.

Become still and allow God's grace to fill you.

God's grace is always present.

Be open and receive what is *always present!*

Death's Duty

Each day of the year, each moment in time, has its uniqueness.

As each moment is honored, it becomes special and flows into the next moment.

It is during this honoring of the moments that we learn to treasure one another.

That is the value of death.

Death has no value but to teach you how important it is to treasure each moment.

Death's duty requires you to take inventory; to assess your moments; to determine how you have dealt with your time and energy in this realm.

Death is not the end of anything except the time you have with others on this earthly plane.

That's why living in the moment, *loving in the moment,* is so important.

When it comes your time to cross over, all that's important is how loving you have been.

That's why it's so important to cultivate love, joy, and happiness.

These are the qualities you take with you.

These are the qualities that develop your soul.

There is nothing else to learn.

Cultivate these qualities and you cultivate the soul.

Death's value lies in honoring life's moments.

ᘓ ᘓ ᘓ

Listen to a Grain of Sand

God's words will come to you if you listen.
Your job is to listen to the words of God in all things.
All things have a way of speaking.
The trees, the flowers and the rocks all have a voice.
Part of your earth training is to learn to hear them.
Think of what a tiny grain of sand could tell you about life!
How did it begin?
Where on the planet did it originate?
How did it get so tiny?
Where has it traveled?
Has it been to the center of the earth?
Did its life begin in our galaxy or was it a part of a fragment that hurtled through deep space?
From what mass of stone did it originate?
How did it cope with being broken from its original mass?
Think of what you could learn from a *single grain of sand!*
As you learn to listen to God through each grain of sand, you become aware of the sacredness in all things.
Listen.
What is God saying to you now?

༺ ༺ ༺

Your Inner Fulcrum

It is perfectly natural to go through times when you feel unsettled.

The energy forces in this realm are elliptical, which means reality is experienced in cycles.

There are seasons on this planet and seasons in your life.

These cycles may *seem* arbitrary, but are really quite orderly.

There are times of clarity and times of confusion; times of being alone and times of being with others; times of being dependent and times of being independent.

Every state of being has its contrast.

That's one of the reasons you came into this realm – to experience duality.

States in this realm are temporary by nature, and as *you* become balanced, these states become less extreme.

That's why it is so important to develop your inner fulcrum, your inner point of balance.

This inner point becomes the place from which you relate to all things.

You develop this point by being quiet and going within.

There will always be times of being unsettled, but you learn to be more comfortable with these times as you develop balance.

Be quiet.

Be still.

Go within and develop your inner point of balance.

Jealousy

Jealousy is simply fear that there is *not enough*.

It is the belief that there are limited quantities of wealth, beauty, poise, or whatever you covet.

Underlying jealousy is the belief that if someone has something you want, it diminishes you.

Jealousy is a belief in limitation.

You think that because they have it, you can't.

To overcome jealousy, decide to believe that everyone else is an extension of you!

Decide to believe that there is an abundance of all things that are good, and that you live in a world with no limits.

As you adopt these beliefs, notice that you can begin to enjoy the qualities in others of which you *used to be* jealous.

Rejoice that a part of you is able to experience wealth, beauty, and poise in a way you hadn't thought of before.

As you begin to appreciate and admire what others have, the veil of separation lifts and you truly experience oneness.

The fear of limitation and jealousy dissipates like dust in the wind.

Instead of jealousy, you experience love.

You cannot experience fear when you are experiencing love.

Without fear, there is no jealousy.

Allow yourself to live in love and enjoy the abundance of all life!

෮෨ ෮෨ ෮෨

Always Assume the Best

What if you decided to always assume the best?

What if you made the decision right now, that no matter what happened, or who was involved, you would always assume the best possible intentions?

If a mistake is made, you assume it's an innocent mistake.

That doesn't mean you don't solve problems, but you don't automatically assume someone is out to "get" you.

When you assume the best, you open doors to receiving positive energy, so that creative solutions present themselves more easily.

When you assume the worst, you get caught in the cycle of negative thinking.

Negative thinking is not productive.

It lowers your energy and zaps your strength.

Notice how tired you are during a binge of negative thinking!

Does assuming the best change the situation?

Maybe not, but it *changes you*.

How you think about a situation is the first step in the process of finding a solution.

Decide to think the best and notice how changing that one assumption changes your entire life.

∾ ∾ ∾

The Irony of Addiction

Addiction is a quest to deal with reality.

The irony of indulging an addiction is that it creates its own false reality, and that false reality becomes preferable to ordinary reality.

The more an addiction is indulged, the more difficult it is to cope with "ordinary" reality.

The problem is that the false reality created by the addiction is not enough.

The addicts' altered consciousness is not "real."

The addicts' altered consciousness is not the holy state sought by mystics, but rather a cruel alternative that leads to the destruction of the mind, body, and spirit.

To overcome an addiction, the addict must become grounded in reality.

As this grounding takes place, the realization will come that reality is indeed holy, and *this holiness* is what the addict *has been seeking* all along.

As the false reality of addiction is released, the sacredness of "ordinary" reality can be embraced.

The real quest is within, learning to embrace ordinary reality in the heart!

The way to let go of addiction is to live every moment in the now, in the gift of what is really "extraordinary" reality.

That reality exists within the extraordinary heart of each one of us!

Creating Your Ideal Self

What are you creating, this day, for yourself?
Courage? Integrity? Honor?
What do you chose to experience in this moment?
Compassion? Tolerance?
Or do you choose anger, frustration, or irritation?
What does it mean to be a co-creator?
Can you create the mountains, the oceans, or the stars?
Can you create who you are?
Who would you create if you could?
What qualities would you give yourself?
What thoughts would you think?
What emotions would you feel?
What talents would you develop?
What skills would you practice?
How would you spend your *inner* time?
How would you spend your *outer* time?
Would you impose limitations on yourself?
How would you begin this process of creating yourself?

Perhaps the place to start is becoming aware of what you have *already created*.

What have you chosen to experience for yourself in this moment?

What is your highest ideal of yourself?

Begin now, with each thought, creating this ideal.

Choose this ideal self *each moment* and you create it.

That's how you co-create, through choice, day-by-day, moment-by-moment, and thought-by-thought, throughout eternity.

What are you creating for yourself *now*?

∾ ∾ ∾

Master Your Life

Learning to focus attention is the first step needed to be in control of your life.

All other choices are based on the ability to master this first step.

If you can't choose what happens to your attention, you can't choose anything else.

Your attention is the pathway of your energy.

Your thoughts are the manifestation of this energy.

That's why becoming aware of your thoughts is so important.

Where your thoughts are, your energies are.

The value of meditation is that it helps you become conscious of your thoughts.

Becoming aware of your thoughts tells you where your attention is.

Becoming aware of your attention tells you where your energy is.

Becoming aware of where your energy is allows you to *choose* whether to keep it where it is or to focus it on something else.

This freedom of choice allows you to control, and therefore to *create*, what you want to manifest in your life.

Master your attention and you master your life.

∽ ∽ ∽

Let God Fill You

You cannot be full of your own ego and expect God to fill you.

What is already full has no room for anything more.

How do you know when ego is taking up your inner space?

The hallmarks of ego are contempt, blame, resentment, frustration, anger, humiliation, and depression.

The ego uses these negative emotions to justify its existence.

The ego surrounds itself with these justifications, like a fortress, digging in so it can play out its warfare.

The ego's motivation is fear.

The ego is the personality's remnant of the animal brain all humans share.

This animal part is important because it keeps the body from being destroyed while on the earth plane.

You must honor this part, which keeps the body alive, but not let it take over your life.

Satisfy its needs so it doesn't overtake you.

Know that who you really are *cannot be destroyed*.

Why are you here in the first place?

If your survival were insured, what would you do?

How would you live?

Let go of the ego's fear and allow God's love to fill you.

When you let that happen, you rise to a whole new level of existence; free from the negative, filled with the positive.

Let God fill you and experience the bliss of your soul's dreams.

❦ ❦ ❦

The Nature of Sunshine

The nature of life is like the nature of sunshine: It's always shining, warming, and healing, somewhere – even when you're not aware of it.

Even on cloudy days, it's still doing its work, steadfast and unrelenting.

As you continue your journey on earth, sometimes you face the sun and sometimes you turn away, but it's always a part of the natural cycle of living.

Think of it!

You could not live here on this planet without the sun, and yet, most of the time you're not even aware of it.

Imagine having your own individual sun inside of you, always shining, giving you constant healing, warmth, and energy.

This energy does its job whether you are aware of it or not. It is always "turned on."

This energy is your inner force, and it is always within you!

Now imagine learning how to harness this energy, how to direct it!

The first step in learning to do this is to become aware that this energy is within you.

How do you want to use this power?

How do you want to direct this energy?

As you do these things, you learn to access the power of God within you.

God's power is shining within you all the time, just like the sunshine!

Help From the Other Side

Remember, you are always being helped from the other side.

There are times when you are aware of that help, and times when you are not.

Think back on events that took place in your life, when you don't know how you got through them.

Your angels were helping you!

That's why there is never a need to fear the future: You never face anything alone.

When you remember to thank your angels for their help, you become more aware of all the help they gave you in the past.

As your gratitude flows out to them, it acts like a magnet and draws their love even closer to you.

As you become aware of your angels' love for you, your life takes on a glorious glow.

This energetic glow becomes a bridge to other peoples' hearts, softening their burdens and lighting their paths.

As you become aware of how you are helped from the other side, you are better able to help those on *this side*.

As you learn to recognize this truth, you glow even brighter with beauty and light.

As you recognize how much you are loved, it's easier to extend love.

Whatever you are thankful for multiplies.

Be thankful for the help you are getting from the other side and watch it grow!

The Portals to the Soul

Each thought you think, each word you speak, each song you sing, is a portal to your soul.

Each vibration extended outward eventually leads back.

Love multiplies.

Fear divides.

That's why every thought of love comes back to you a thousandfold.

Every thought of fear diminishes you.

Think a thought of love about someone.

Feel how that loving thought of someone else *enriches you!*

Your own energy glows with goodness as you send love to another.

Now think a fearful thought, a thought of lack, of poverty, of illness.

Feel your *own body* contract with the negative force of this fearful thought.

The person who you affect the most with your thoughts *is you!*

You *hurt yourself* with negative emotions.

Holding on to negative emotions is simply your soul's plea for growth.

Practice releasing the negative and embracing the positive.

Practice.

Your soul's growth depends on this.

The Symphony of Your Soul

There is a song inside of you waiting to emerge.

Only you can sing this song.

Only you can perform this melody.

You are the *only instrument* tuned to this frequency.

Think of it!

In the entire universe, you have a song like no other!

Until you sing your song, the symphony of the universe is incomplete.

You are important beyond your ability to measure.

You can't measure the value of your own song because you don't know how it sounds from the far reaches of infinity.

There is no end to the effects your voice has on the universe and everything in it.

The vibration of who you are creates, whether you intend to or not.

That's why your creation is so important.

What do you want to create?

What do you want your song to be?

You are singing a song, so you might as well tune your instrument.

Sing your song so that it echoes with joy throughout the universe!

Creating Your Life

What are you creating in your life?

Are you creating joy, harmony, or peace?

Are you creating discord, confusion, or unrest?

Every moment you are alive, you are creating, whether you're aware of it or not.

You create with your words, the expressions on your face, the way you walk down the street, the way you drive your car.

You create with positive thoughts of love and support, or with negative thoughts of fear and jealousy.

You create with the very nature of who you are: A spiritual being seeking growth within the earthly realms.

Creating discord is easy.

Think of a classroom full of unruly nine-year-olds.

A single mischievous glance can send the entire class into an uproar!

Creating harmony is easy, too.

Think of the power a simple smile has on a tired parent rushing through the grocery store.

These are important, profound creations that impact your life – and the lives of others – daily.

Become aware of the life you want, and then begin creating it, thought-by-thought, word-by-word, and deed-by-deed.

If you are not creating your life, who is?

What life are *you* creating?

෨ ෨ ෨

Stop the Struggle

Notice how much easier your life is when you stop struggling.

That doesn't mean you give up; it means you give up *fighting* your way through life.

Struggling is simply another word for fighting.

As you give up the energy of the fight, you have much more energy to create.

Many live in a state of inner war, even when there is no outer war to battle.

Some people are only motivated to use their energy for fighting.

But the energy of the battlefield is inappropriate when the war is really in your heart.

Even warriors must learn when it is appropriate to be peaceful.

Notice the shift of energy as you find that place of peace within yourself.

Does anyone really win in a fight?

Fighting corrupts the heart and diminishes the soul.

You can only give to others what you have in your heart.

Develop peace in your heart and there will be no struggle.

Access the calm resolve within and notice how much stronger you are.

Give your struggles to God.

Let God transform the energy for you, and experience the strength and power of peace.

෭ඓ ෭ඓ ෭ඓ

What Reality Are You Creating?

Peace, prosperity, and happiness: How can you have one without the others?

Positive states contribute to every other positive state, just as negative states contribute to every other negative state.

Every thought contributes to one of these states.

The first step in creating your own reality is becoming aware of your thoughts and directing them in a positive manner.

Sometimes it may seem as if you have no control over your thoughts.

You may get caught in a downward spiral of thinking before you realize what's happening.

The moment you realize you are having a negative thought, it is crucial to stop yourself and immediately redirect your thinking!

Negative thinking serves no purpose at all!

Negative thoughts just lead to more negative thoughts!

It is within your power to choose to end the negative spiral.

Do you realize the fantastic power you have to change the course of your thinking?

How do you choose to use this awesome power?

What reality are you creating?

If it's not the reality you want, begin to change it now, thought by thought.

Don't "Should" on Yourself

Are you "shoulding" on yourself?

Would you like to give up your "have tos?"

What would your life be like if you had no "shoulds" or "have tos?"

What would you do with your time if you didn't "have to" do anything?

What would you do with your energy if you had no "shoulds?"

When you become aware of how you would spend your time and energy without your "shoulds" and "have tos," you'll become aware of where your resistance lies.

The paradox is that your resistance fuels the "shoulds" and "have tos."

These then become limitations.

As you continue to resist these areas, your life fills up with limitations and your energy is blocked.

When you quit resisting, you can fulfill your obligations with peace and joy, and the blocks and limitations automatically dissolve.

As you free yourself from the internal warfare of resistance, you open yourself up to the freedom of choice.

Look at your "shoulds" and "have tos" as signs of internal warfare.

As you develop peace within yourself, this peace radiates and becomes blessings to those around you.

See your "shoulds" as signposts of internal transformations that haven't yet taken place.

When you stop "shoulding" on yourself, your whole life will transform into one series of miracles after another.

Free Love

The same God who is watching over you is also watching over your loved ones.

The same God who is watching over your loved ones is also watching over those you *think* you *don't* love.

Why would you withhold your love from someone God is watching over?

Do you know better than God whom to love and whom not to love?

Finding reasons not to love is just another way of justifying resentment.

As you withhold your love, you create backlogs of energy.

These energy blocks dam up your system and cause all kinds of "power outages."

That's why when you let go of resentment you feel so free: You've broken up an internal love block so that divine creative energy can flow through you once again.

God does not stop the energy flow; you do.

You stop the energy flow when you stop the love flow.

What are you afraid will happen if you love another?

Extend love to just one aspect of another whom you used to resent.

Allow the energy to shift from resentment to love.

Imagine what it would feel like to have no resentment.

Imagine allowing your love to flow freely.

Allow yourself to feel the power of God's unconditional love flowing through you, just as it flows through those you *used to think* you didn't love!

That's free love!

Contrast Without Negativity

Contrast keeps life interesting.

Duality - the yin and the yang - is what you came to this realm to experience.

Contrast allows you to explore your diverse potentials.

Some people, however, are so addicted to drama that they create chaos rather than risk experiencing boredom.

That's one reason some people so easily engage in warfare: It's exciting.

But contrast exists everywhere; it doesn't need to be artificially manufactured.

Duality can be as simple as the difference between a smile and a frown, or as intense as the difference between love and hate.

As you learn to appreciate the positive nature of contrast, its joyous aspects multiply.

The thunderous roar of a cascading waterfall, the soothing rhythm of soft waves on the shore - both are contrasting sounds, yet neither is negative.

Would you know what faith is if you hadn't experienced fear?

How much contrast do you need to experience in order to be motivated to grow?

How much pain do you need to go through before you realize you can grow just as well through joy?

It's just as easy to learn from tasting the difference between salty and sweet, as it is between sour and bitter.

Learn to experience contrast between the positive aspects of life and the need to experience the negative aspects diminishes.

∾ ∾ ∾

A Sleeping Vacation

Consider taking a sleeping vacation.

A sleeping vacation consists of time you arrange so that you can sleep as long as you desire.

Sleep is one of the most underrated aspects of life.

Levels of consciousness exist naturally during sleep that otherwise only exist during meditation or self-hypnosis.

You can actually *become aware* at those levels of consciousness while you are "asleep."

With practice, you can learn to visit other realms, communicate with other souls, and accomplish a great deal of extraordinary work in these altered states.

Dreams can be prophetic, healing, and problem solving.

Dreams can provide information that you couldn't get any other way.

There are resources available to you in sleep that seem almost magical.

Sleep is one of the surest ways to center and become grounded.

The lack of sleep may not kill you, but it will certainly destroy your sanity.

Notice the difference in how you feel when you get enough sleep and when you're sleep-deprived.

As you learn to become aware of how valuable your sleep is, you may decide it makes perfect sense to take a "sleeping vacation."

∾ ∾ ∾

Internal Dialogue

The way that you speak internally has a profound effect on your entire being.

Your unconscious mind has no filter.

It can't discriminate between what is real and what isn't.

Your unconscious mind is like a small child; it believes everything you tell it.

When you say to yourself, "This job is killing me," your unconscious mind believes this, literally.

That's why you tend to get sick when you're in stressful situations.

You take that stress to the "nth" degree and it becomes magnified.

A more accurate statement would be, "This job is tiring," or, "This job requires too many hours," etc.

These statements are not only closer to the truth, but cause less stress in your life.

Your entire being goes into the "fight or flight" response when you tell yourself that *something is killing you.*

Your unconscious mind doesn't understand figurative language.

Experience how much better your whole body feels when you change, "These shoes are killing me," to, "These shoes are hurting my feet."

As you become aware of how you speak to yourself, you also become aware of how you speak to others.

Remember, kindness starts from within.

Be kind with your inner words and it becomes natural to be kind with your outer ones.

The Greatest Experience

As you open your inner self to the healing energy of God's love, your entire world begins to take on a fascinating beauty.

The world begins to glisten with the glow of life.

The iridescent shimmer of energy begins to reveal itself in all things.

Your senses take on an almost magical ability to perceive the beauty of creation.

The sense of separation diminishes and you experience oneness with the universe.

This is not a myth.

This is *not* just available to a select few.

This experience is available to everyone who seeks it and is a *natural aspect* of the journey within.

This manifestation is the unfolding of your spiritual nature into the physical realms.

You can't *make* it happen.

You *allow* it to happen.

As you become aware of your own blessed nature, all around you becomes blessed.

This results as a natural expansion of your energy field.

You become aware of God's love.

You become aware that God's love is *inside* of you.

You become aware that God's love is *outside* of you.

Your awareness of this love lifts the veil of separation and allows you to experience oneness with all.

As you open to God's love, you open, *period*.

What greater experience is there?

∾ ∾ ∾

Loving From the Inside Out

How is it that you are able to recognize love?

What inside you knows what love is?

In order for you to recognize what love is on the *outside*, there must already be love *within you* that you can use as a measure.

This same principal applies to truth, beauty, integrity, and all positive attributes.

You must have these qualities within you; that's how you know what they are.

The best way to experience them outside of you is to develop them from the inside out.

If you want more love in your life, develop the love you have within yourself.

Cultivate the feeling of love until it is so strong that it radiates from you like light from a glistening diamond.

Cultivate joy so that you shine like a brilliant flame in the darkness.

Experience what it feels like to love you!

Extend this love outward and let it encompass *one thing* that exists outside of you.

It can be anything of your choice: A cloud, a flower, an object of your choice.

As you extend your love to include this object, notice how your love grows.

Practice this until your first thoughts of yourself are of love.

This practice will help you manifest love, so that your loving energy encompasses all.

Fear is a Teacher

Experiencing fear is a natural part of being human.

Everyone experiences fear at one time or another.

Bravery is *not* a result of having *no fear*.

Bravery is the result of *having fear* and then proceeding in spite of it.

How can you be brave, how can you learn courage, if you have no fear?

Fear is the element that allows you to *develop courage*.

Your job is to develop enough inner strength so that when fear presents itself, you aren't overpowered.

The sooner you recognize fear for what it is, the sooner you can use it to help you.

Fear has a positive intention for you.

It may want to protect you.

It may want to make you strong.

Some people need the adrenaline rush of fear to become motivated.

If you begin to see fear in this way and begin to understand what it wants you to learn, its power over you will diminish.

Fear only exists for you until you learn its lesson.

The question is not, "How do I get rid of fear?"

The question is, "What does fear want for me?"

Look at fear as a teacher, and ask what it wants you to learn.

∾ ∾ ∾

Love Yourself So You Can Love Others

One of the most important things you can do is love yourself.

It sounds simple, and it is, but sometimes it's not easy.

There is a difference between self-love and selfish love.

It is imperative that you love yourself, because only you *know yourself* on a level that *requires* unconditional love.

Only you know your inner self, your foibles, your inadequacies, and your character defects.

When you can learn to love yourself in spite of all your less-than-stellar qualities, you can learn to love others; that's why cultivating self-love is crucial.

Self-love opens your energetic centers and allows universal love (energy) to flow freely through you.

The lack of self-love creates blocks in these energy centers and prevents the free flow of divine love through you.

Begin to love yourself by focusing on one aspect of yourself that you enjoy.

Focus on anything about yourself that you appreciate.

What is one aspect or characteristic you value about yourself?

Honor that aspect.

Allow that honor to grow.

This establishes integrity.

Integrity is simply holding yourself in high esteem.

As you do this, your love grows.

As your love grows for yourself, it grows for others.

That's why loving yourself is so important.

Whom Should You Trust?

Trust is one of the most powerful tools you can develop.

You don't need to trust *another person.*

You don't need to trust your lover.

You don't need to trust your parents or your teachers.

You don't need to trust *anyone* other than the divine within.

Trusting another sets you up for betrayal.

Trusting another is just a way of giving your power to others.

However, your trust is *always safe* when you give it to God.

Your trust is not only safe when you give it to God; it is magnified.

As you give your trust to divine energy, it multiplies.

As you give your trust to the divine flame of God's light, your own light shines brighter.

You begin to trust yourself more because you begin to understand that God is working *through you.*

As you begin to trust this, you begin to trust that God is working through others as well.

You are not alone in this universe and never have been.

The loving support of God's energy is always with you.

Trust, and experience the freedom of knowing you are loved.

෨ ෨ ෨

The Magical, Miraculous You

You have the capacity to experience fabulous mystical encounters.

Mystical experiences are available to everyone, not just a limited few, as you may have been taught to believe.

You don't have to be "chosen."

You get to choose.

Once you decide that you are worthy of God's love, you open your heart to receive divine grace.

An open heart is the only requirement.

You are the *only one* who can make this choice.

This ability to choose is the reason you have free will.

Do you choose to open your heart or not?

Go deep inside and discover how it feels to open your heart.

Feel the safety of giving your heart to divine love.

Trust that the universe has your highest good in mind.

Allow your energies to open.

Feel the power of God's love flowing through you.

As you accept divine energy into your heart, it multiplies and you become a conduit for heavenly grace.

Your energies are transformed from the inside out.

Belief becomes knowledge.

Knowledge becomes experience.

You are a mystical experience.

Choose to keep your heart open, and allow your mystical transformation to unfold.

This is the beginning of creating miracles!

∾ ∾ ∾

Open Your Mystical Channels

The only difference between mystical moments and ordinary moments is your *perception* of them.

As you begin to perceive the incredible magical nature of all events, in all communications, you begin to perceive that *nothing is ordinary.*

There is just as much magic in the communication between you and your mother-in-law as there is between you and your angel.

There is just as much magic in learning a foreign language as there is in interpreting a dream.

There is just as much magic in ice-skating as there is in astral traveling.

When you learn to value each moment, each event, each manifestation of energy, you learn that there is no separation between "ordinary" experiences and mystical experiences.

It's not any more difficult to communicate with a flower than it is to communicate with your teenager.

The magic that makes a tree grow is the same magic that makes your heart beat.

Each of us lives an *extraordinary life.*

The only difference is that the mystic *knows* how extraordinary "normal" life is!

Open your mystical channels by recognizing the value of each "ordinary" moment!

∽ ∽ ∽

God's Thoughts and You

Substance is simply the concentration of thought.

Thought is conscious energy.

Conscious energy develops as you become aware that you can direct your thoughts.

As you consciously direct you thoughts, you increase your *personal power*.

As you align your thoughts with divine energy, you increase your *universal power*.

Both personal and universal powers are necessary to create miracles.

Personal power helps you make the decision (direct your thoughts) to align with divine energy in the first place.

Universal power is what flows through you when this alignment is accomplished.

This is how you become a vehicle for God's love.

As you make the conscious decision to align your energies with divine energies, you open your internal energy centers to heaven's blessings.

You are transformed as heavenly grace flows through you.

The more you allow God's will to replace *your* will, the more personal *and* universal powers you are able to manifest.

Since the power of God's thoughts transcend personal and universal powers, this alignment allows you to become the vehicle for the manifestation of miracles.

What miracles do *you* want to manifest?

God is in the Quiet

Don't be afraid of the quiet.

Silence does not mean you are alone.

Silence is a *gift* to remind you that there is a greater reality beyond what you can hear.

There are many worlds beyond what you can hear.

Sound gives you the illusion that you are not alone because it is an audible manifestation of activity.

Experiencing quiet allows you to go through the doorway into experiencing stillness.

Stillness opens the doorway to God.

You cannot hear God when you are listening to something else.

That something else may be external or it may be internal.

Internal noise may occupy just as much of your attention as external noise.

You cannot *force* your internal noise to stop.

As you notice it without judgment, the internal chatter diminishes.

It diminishes because you're not giving it power with your judgment.

Judgment is another form of resistance.

The more you resist, the more energy you give to the object of your resistance.

Stillness has no resistance.

God has no resistance.

There is no need to resist the quiet because that is where God is waiting to speak to you.

Turn on Your Inner Fountain of Joy

Divine energy works through you in a way that it cannot work through any one else in the universe.

You are a unique vessel through which God can work.

Your job is to refine your vessel so that even more divine energy can manifest through you.

This refinement naturally brings you into alignment with God's energy.

As you appreciate the beauty of who you are, your beauty grows.

Your natural beauty unfolds as you honor it.

The more you cultivate this inner beauty, the easier it is for God to work through you.

Turn on your inner fountain of joy.

No other waters can flow through your fountain, and no one else can turn it on.

The more you rejoice in who you are, the more able you are to rejoice in others.

The glory of God's energy working through you begins to touch those around you in ways that are beyond your earthly understanding.

You become a conduit of God's love.

This is what being a servant of God truly means.

This servitude is not a sacrifice; it is a privilege!

This privilege can only manifest through *your* personal energy system.

Turn on your inner fountain of joy and become God's true servant.

The Unseen Forces

You receive much help that is unseen.

The next time you narrowly miss harm, the next time you are dazzled by the beauty of a sunset, the next time a bird's song thrills your ears, say, "*Thank you.*"

The more you appreciate God's gifts around you, the more they multiply in your life.

The more you acknowledge the unseen forces working in your life, the more obvious they will become.

If you had an inkling of how much *you are adored*, your whole life would change.

You may not believe you're worthy of adoration because you identify with the physical, egotistical aspects of your nature.

Those are temporary aspects that you have chosen to wear like a cloak.

Why would the unseen, holy forces adore your clothes?

The holy forces see beyond what you are wearing and into the innermost aspects of who are really you.

Who you really are is worthy of the holiest praise.

This inner, real you, is the truth you *must* get to know!

As you get to know this true you, you will begin to see it in others.

As you see it in others, you become aware of it in the unseen.

Appreciate the help you receive from the unseen, and it will be easier for you to see!

∽ ∽ ∽

The World Starts with You

What kind of world exists outside you?

Is it a kind, loving, peaceful world?

Or is it a mean, cold, hateful world?

You can change the world *outside* by changing the world *inside*.

Begin by changing your mean thoughts.

Mean thoughts on the inside translate into war on the outside.

Catch your thinking.

Make a game of it.

Decide what kind of world you want to live in, both on the inside and on the outside, and begin creating it on an internal level.

If you want to live with beauty, kindness, and forgiveness, begin by catching your negative thoughts and changing them into positive ones.

Your world really does start with you.

When Christ said, "Love thy neighbor," he wasn't kidding.

Why is that still a revolutionary idea?

It's revolutionary because there is a natural *human* tendency to be negative and territorial.

The key to transformation is to consciously change your negative thoughts.

No one else can do this inner work.

Now ask yourself again, what kind of world exists outside of you?

The God Messages

God speaks to every single person.

God is in your ears, your heart, your mouth, and your mind.

God's voice is echoing through you constantly; it's just that you usually aren't quiet enough to hear.

God doesn't *require* you to be quiet; it's simply a natural condition that exists in order to hear Him.

God's message doesn't depend on sound; God's message depends on attitude.

As you cultivate an attitude of willingness to hear, you open yourself to receiving heavenly messages.

God speaks in as many ways as there are people.

Think of it.

Billions and billions of divine messages!

What is God's message for you?

God's message may come as a glint of sunshine on a fluttering leaf.

It may come as a sparkling drop of rain on a round pebble.

It may come as a shy smile from a complete stranger.

It may come as a lover's embrace on a quiet evening.

Pay attention.

Be still.

Notice the God messages in your life.

ᘓ ᘓ ᘓ

The Consciousness of Death

Death can never be fully understood in this realm because it exists at a different level of consciousness.

Just as the experiences in dreams can never be completely explained in the waking state, the experiences you have on the "other side" can never be completely explained on "this side."

As you cross over to the other side, the perceptual shift you undergo is huge.

You only perceive this perceptual shift as being "dead" because the veil that separates the realms is so heavy that communication becomes difficult.

It's easier to communicate with those in that realm when you allow yourself to go into an altered state of consciousness, through meditation, self-hypnosis or dreams.

Communication with the other side eases the fear and softens the grief you associate with death.

There is no "end."

Death is not final.

The death of people you care about is a loss to you, but not to those who have crossed over.

Death feels like loss because you are bound to the levels of consciousness associated with the waking realms.

This is why death is like a dream: It can be beautiful, glorious, mysterious, and impossible to explain in the earthly realm.

Learn to honor the mysteries of death and a natural understanding of it will develop within you.

A Question of Change

It is okay to question.

It is okay to change your mind.

It is okay to be uncertain.

Doubt is a natural state that you experience because you're human.

As a human, you exist in a state of duality.

You go back and forth between certainty and doubt, between knowing and not knowing.

It's important to *bless* each state you are in whether you consider it positive or negative, whether you like it or not.

Blessing each state helps you release it.

Blessing each state helps you bless yourself.

If you can recognize that each state is necessary for your personal development, you can bless it and let it go.

Don't try to hold onto a particular state of being; it's going to change anyway.

The more willing you are to experience change, the easier it will be for you to grow.

Trying to keep the status quo causes energy to get stuck.

You dam up your energy fields with fear of change.

Having questions implies that you are in the midst of change.

It's wonderful and fulfilling to find answers, just don't try to hang on to them.

Let your answers lead to *new* questions, knowing that there is nothing to fear!

The Power of Joy

The power of joy cannot be overestimated.

Joy has the power to transform like no other earthly energy.

Joy clears away negative blocks with astounding swiftness.

It cleanses more thoroughly than any other kind of energy.

That's why cultivating joy is paramount to spiritual growth.

Joy is earth's precursor to heavenly bliss.

The cultivation of joy allows the natural unfolding of positive energies: Faith, honesty, integrity, loyalty, selflessness and all constructive forces.

The glory you experience in one area of your life naturally spreads to others, like sunlight rippling on an endless ocean.

There are as many avenues of joy as there are points of perception, and all these avenues lead to divine transformations.

Joy is the portal through which divine energy works.

As you open yourself to experience joy, you open yourself to experience God.

What greater power is there?

໑ ໑ ໑

Grief

Grief is not to be resolved, grief is to be endured.

There is no comfort for a child who has lost its mother.

There is no comfort for a mother who has lost her child.

This deep sorrow cannot be mollified.

This sadness cannot be cured.

This grief must be lived.

Just as you cannot stop the oceans from crashing on the shores, you cannot stop the waves of sorrow crashing in your heart.

There is nothing to do.

Tears won't wash away grief.

Words provide no relief.

Sleep becomes an absent lover.

There is no peace, no warmth, and no comfort.

As one learns to crawl through this awful pain, there is no desire to see light again.

This overpowering, unending darkness is something we all share.

We have all been there.

Which is why a smile, a hug, a tiny kindness should become your goals: When you can, when you're ready, when grief softens its hold.

Even though at times you may wish that you, too, were dead.

Grief endured is part of life lived.

∾ ∾ ∾

Hatred is a Twisted Cry for Love

Hatred is built on layers of frustration, and frustration is the continual inability to receive love.

You may think the only way to feel satisfied is to strike back at another.

Spite is really a cover-up for hurt feelings.

You may believe that if you hurt another it will lessen your own ache.

You may think another's pain will lessen yours.

But when you hurt another your own pain is multiplied.

Bitterness develops in the ruts that hatred creates.

Forgiveness sweeps away these ruts like footprints washed away by gentle waves.

It is the *self* that must be forgiven.

The self must be forgiven for allowing negative thoughts to create such ruts in the first place.

When you love your *self*, there is no room for hatred; there is no way frustration can develop, because the flow of love is complete.

Find ways to love your self and the grooves of hatred won't have a chance to develop.

There is no need to cry for outer love, because the need will have been met with *inner* love.

That's where love comes from in the first place!

There's no room for hate when you are filled with love!

The Sacred Realm of Dreams

Dreams are portals into the mystic's realm.

Dreams provide the vehicle through which you navigate the world of symbols, metaphors, and signs.

Your job is to master the vehicle and interpret the symbols.

The more you practice this sacred task the more clarity you receive through the dream world.

Dreams allow you to access parts of yourself you may need to exercise and explore.

You can confront your fears, face your enemies, and conquer your deepest weakness in the safety of your own bed.

What greater tool for spiritual exercise could you ask?

Dreams can reveal secrets about you that no other realm can.

Dreams allow you the safety to ask questions that you would only ask of your inner self.

The more you pay attention to your dreams, the more you honor them, the easier it is to learn their language.

What would you like to know?

What questions would you like answered?

Ask to be shown the answer to one question before you go to sleep.

Keep asking every night until you are shown the answer in a dream.

You may need to ask the same question for a period of time, but the answer will come.

If you don't understand the answer, ask for clarity.

Don't waste your sleep.

It's some of the most valuable time in your life.

❧ ❧ ❧

Develop Love's Peace

A peaceful outer life is no guarantee of a peaceful *inner* life.

There will always be times of upset, strife, and chaos in the external world.

As you develop calmness, peace, and security within, you naturally project these qualities into the outer world.

As you develop peace within, you radiate it outwards.

Strength is inherent in true peace.

One cannot experience true peace without strength.

There is no peace in weakness.

Weakness is the product of fear, and fear knows neither peace nor strength.

The false sense of power fear produces is really panic, which is short-lived.

Fear's lover is more fear.

It doesn't know how to exist except to feed on itself.

Notice as you pray, "Give me the strength to be calm," that before the calm comes a sea of love.

As love settles into the center of your being, you experience calm, security, and strength.

Love is the center of the unmovable quiet within.

Christ said, "Love your enemies."

That admonition wasn't for the benefit of your enemies; it was for the benefit of *you*.

When you experience love you experience peace.

Develop love's inner peace and the outside turmoil will cease to trouble you.

How to Create Miracles

The closer you are to God, the more beauty you see in your life.

The more you tune into the higher, creative vibrations, the more you tune into joy, confidence, and peace.

You tend to see what is *easier* for you to perceive.

That's why cultivating your *inner* beauty, which is really divine beauty, naturally allows you to become aware of outer beauty.

As you recognize the Divine within it becomes easier to recognize the Divine without.

Begin to think of yourself as holy, because in truth, *you are*.

As you acknowledge this holiness, it grows.

God has blessed *your* soul just as surely as He has blessed the soul you most admire on the planet.

There is no hierarchy in God's blessings.

God does not pour love upon one and not another.

It is *your earthly job* to utilize God's love and blessings.

Be thankful.

Be joyous.

Your gratitude and joy open the door to utilize God's creative energy.

As you let joy fill you on the inside it flows outside and colors everything with luminescent beauty.

Cultivate joy and you cultivate life.

It is your earthly job to allow the divine energies of beauty and love to flow through you.

This is what brings you closer to God.

This is how you create miracles!

Be Your Own Mystic!

The voice *within you* speaks the loudest.

There is no other voice in the universe that has the power of your inner voice.

That's why in order for *you to change* you must change your inner voice.

Only when the inner voice agrees with the outer voice is true resonance achieved.

This resonance allows true communication to occur; your inner voice and your outer voice agreeing.

Your inner voice may not speak to you in words.

It may communicate to you with feelings, visions, or metaphors.

Each form of communication is as unique as each individual.

You are the only one who can receive this information because it was designed uniquely for you.

There may be times when it's easier for you to accept this communication.

You may notice it has a certain rhythm.

Once you become aware of this rhythm and tune into it, receiving will be easier.

"Ask and ye shall receive."

Practice and it becomes natural.

Listen to the voice within and become *your own* mystic.

~ ~ ~

The Imperfect Body Helps Perfect the Soul

The body will never be perfect.

The body is designed to allow you to express yourself in the physical realm.

One of your jobs is to evolve the body so that you can bring more highly refined, spiritual energy into the physical.

If you brought *all* of your energies from the spiritual realm into the physical body, you would blow its circuits.

Your body is designed to help you create, develop, and explore this three-dimensional reality.

Your body is to be enjoyed, treasured, and honored.

As you learn to develop your energies within the body, you will learn to consciously create and heal the physical form.

You are doing it now; you simply don't give it conscious attention.

Inner joy creates a smile.

Sadness creates tears.

Love boosts the immune system.

Grief weakens it.

What kind of body do you want to express *through?*

What are you learning through your body that you couldn't learn any other way?

What would you like to change, if anything, about your body?

The body will never be perfect, but it *is* designed to help you perfect your soul.

Receiving the Divine Voice

It's important that your life is filled with your own words.

No other words can have the same impact on your life as those that come through your own being.

Ask yourself, "What do I need to hear?"

What do you need to hear to help you on your journey?

What do you need to hear to help others on their journeys?

Allow yourself time to listen.

Create the quiet in which to hear.

Be a still channel so that knowledge can flow through you.

Let yourself receive the divine voice.

Be still and listen.

What are your words telling you?

As you listen, the words speak louder.

Create the time and the quiet so that you can be a channel for the divine voice.

The Value of Time

What is the value of time?

Time is the medium through which you experience events.

Without time, you would experience all events at once.

Time allows you the opportunity to process and assimilate information, experience, and wisdom.

Time allows you to learn the value of love.

Time allows you the opportunity to let go of fear.

Time allows you to experience the physical form because time is the element in which energy becomes fixed.

As you learn to manage time, you learn to manage energy.

Time itself is not truly fixed.

You develop the ability to flex exterior time as you develop the ability to flex interior time.

You develop this flexibility by being *conscious* in the present moment.

As you bring your energies into focus in present time, your ability to control the past and the future increases.

You change your perception of the past as you focus your attention on the present.

Time's value depends on how you use it.

How are you using your time?

෴ ෴ ෴

Where Miracles are Born

Is your inside world aligned with your outside world?

Are you able to manifest the serenity, joy, and blessings on the outside that you experience on the inside?

What is your inner world like?

What do you *want* it to be like?

It's important to become aware of your private realms, because this is where manifesting miracles begins.

Outer change begins *within*.

You must first have a *thought* in order to create it.

You must have *inner order* to manifest outer order.

Become aware of what's going on in your inner world.

If you are preoccupied with other peoples' outer worlds, how can you create your own?

What is the difference between their outer world and yours?

What is the difference between their inner world and yours?

Notice how outer energy is influenced by inner energy.

Notice how both inner and outer worlds change as you change your thinking.

Which world is most important to you?

If you want to create miracles on the outside, begin creating miracles within.

Your inner worlds are where miracles are born.

∽ ∽ ∽

The Love of Labor

There is no such thing as menial work.

All labor has value when it is infused with love.

Imagine putting love into whatever you do.

The energy of love actually goes into the work and manifests into the product.

Emotion itself is a form of energy.

The contrast of emotions is one of the things you are in this realm to experience.

A signpost of spiritual growth is what *you do* with emotional energy.

What kind of emotional energy do you want to develop?

You have the ability to practice cultivating this emotional energy as you "work," regardless of what kind of work you do.

Work is simply a way of being productive.

As you work, practice cultivating the energy of your choice.

What would happen if every part of every machine, engine, computer, hamburger, and French fry were infused with love?

The world would be entirely different in wondrous ways if everyone remembered to complete every act with a thought of love.

Cultivating love is a way of creating heaven on earth.

What better way of cultivating love than through work?

Work isn't menial.

You make it menial by not valuing the time you put into it.

Put love into your work and it becomes priceless!

Awaken Consciously

It is important to become conscious as soon as you awaken in the morning.

Choose a thought upon which you would like to focus.

Choose something that is concise and meaningful.

It may be something simple like, "Thank you, God."

Focusing your attention immediately upon awakening helps to align your energies and center yourself in God.

As you continue this practice, you learn to manage your energies.

After all, your energies begin to manifest in the material realm with your first thought.

Becoming conscious of what you are thinking is the first step in developing free will.

Free will is your ability to choose.

Becoming conscious aligns you with the power to choose.

If you forget and become distracted, as we all do, simply bring your attention back to your first thought.

If you don't choose your first thought consciously, you unconsciously allow your energies to drift and scatter.

You will not know on what your energies are focusing and will have trouble managing your personal power.

Practice awakening consciously and this awareness will enhance the rest of your life!

൮ ൮ ൮

Problems Don't Have Power, You Do!

Begin to see all problems as if *they were created*.

Think of problems as difficulties that are designed specifically to enhance *your* spiritual skills.

Think of difficulties in your life as puzzles designed for you to solve.

These problems are designed to help you flex your spiritual muscles and manage your energies in this realm.

Problems must be worked out in this realm in order to facilitate spiritual growth.

You came here to evolve.

What better way to evolve than growing through your problems?

Particular problems are in your life because you need to develop particular skills to overcome them.

Problems may also be in your life so that you can teach others how to solve similar ones.

Sometimes it's not a matter of "solving" problems; it's a matter of *rising above them*.

Look at every problem as an opportunity to flex your spiritual muscles.

As you look at life this way, you take your power back from the problem.

Problems don't have power, *you do*.

Learn to use your power and you will see problems in an entirely different way.

When the Body Doesn't Heal

What is the force that heals?

How do you connect with this healing energy?

Is this energy inside of you or outside of you?

Is healing physical, emotional, intellectual, or spiritual?

How do you know when you're healed?

Sometimes *spiritual growth* is *required* when the body doesn't heal.

Sometimes, on a higher level of existence, the soul chooses to experience illness or injury because it forces spiritual evolution.

When you cannot use the physical body, you are required to use the emotional, intellectual, and spiritual bodies.

Illness and injury are not a matter of retribution, blame, or punishment.

They are opportunities to develop aspects of yourself that you might otherwise neglect.

Sometimes the question is not, "How do I heal?" but, "What am I learning by *not* healing?"

Ask the illness what it wants you to know.

Ask the injury what it wants for you.

Ask what it needs to be healed.

When you look at illness and injury as opportunities for growth, you'll begin to see healing in a completely new way, a way that makes miracles possible.

Your Influence on the World

There is no such thing as living a life alone.

You cannot exist without affecting others, and others cannot exist without affecting you.

Everyone affects everyone.

The real question is, "What effects do you *want* to have?"

What kind of influence do you want to be?

Everyone, everything, exerts an influence.

The tiniest leaf can block the sun's burning rays.

One smile can divert a tyrant.

Ask yourself whom and what influences *you* the most.

Whom and what do *you* influence the most?

Even if you never open your mouth, even if you never look at another, you are an influence.

You breathe air, you drink water, you eat food, you wear clothes; you exist.

Your existence on this planet exerts influence because your personal energy exerts influence.

This influence is power.

Once you become aware of this power you can use it.

Every soul has power.

There is no such thing as a powerless life.

A tiny baby who has lived but a short time on this planet has an enormous influence on everyone whose life it touched.

Sometimes the shortest lives have the most influence.

What kind of influence do *you* have?

∽ ∽ ∽

Your Sacred Blueprint

What does your sacred blueprint have in store for you?

What skills did you decide to develop while visiting the earthly realms this time around?

What qualities attracted you to your mother?

What can you learn from her that you couldn't learn from anyone else?

What qualities attracted you to your father?

What can you learn from him that you couldn't learn from anyone else?

What attracted you to your siblings?

If you have no siblings, what can you learn from that?

What are you teaching others?

Who influences you the most in your life at this time?

What is the main thing you want to accomplish during this incarnation?

What is the most important thing you would like others to know about you?

You have a *sacred blueprint* that was developed on the other side that has the answers to these questions and more.

Your job in this realm becomes easier and more fulfilling as you become aware of the details in this blueprint.

This knowledge helps focus your energies so that you can achieve specific goals.

Seeing this holy picture helps you understand difficult relationships, release negative behavior patterns, and let go of limiting thinking.

Discover *your* blueprint so that you can fulfill its sacred design.

ও৺ ও৺ ও৺

The Softness of Acceptance

Sometimes there are no satisfactory answers.
Sometimes life makes no sense.
Sometimes you must sit with unknowing.
It may seem as if everything you have ever known has left you.
Simple numbers don't compute.
The earth isn't round anymore.
There is no reason to eat.
There is no reason *not* to eat.
There is no reason.
As you sit with this unknowing and stop *trying* to figure things out, a slow comfort begins.
If you don't turn to bitterness to escape the unknowing, a softness develops.
This is the softness of acceptance.
It will gradually envelope you if you don't fight it.
Acceptance is coming to terms with the unknowing.
You learn to live through the traumas of having your beliefs destroyed.
You learn to sit within, and walk through a nonsensical world.
Eventually, you discover gravity again.
You discover that if you drop something, it falls to the earth.
There are natural laws.
Order does exist.
Until you come *again* to the place of unknowing and must learn to accept all over again.

Beyond the Mind

The mind wants a job.
The mind always wants to be doing *something*.
That's why it worries.
When involved in worry, it thinks it's doing something *important*.

What the mind is really doing is wasting its energy.

True knowledge and wisdom come to you from *beyond* the mind.

Eventually the mind gets exhausted from racing around so much and in a nanosecond, it's quiet.

In that moment of stillness, the voice of God is able to penetrate the denseness of thinking.

At that point, you receive inspiration.

That is the point at which spontaneous, mystical experiences occur.

The mind has to wear itself out so it can be quiet enough to listen.

When the mind needs something to focus its energy on, give it a mantra.

Give the mind a holy scripture or a positive phrase to keep it busy so it won't occupy itself with negative thoughts or worry.

If you keep the mind busy with holy or positive thoughts, mystical experiences are more likely to occur when stillness happens.

Since the mind wants to be doing something, give it something valuable to do.

Give your mind the job of thinking positive, creative thoughts, so that when it takes a break from its job, you will experience the vibration to receive the mysteries of the universe!

The Antidote to Stress

When you forget to trust, a tightness develops in your chest.

When you forget to trust, all the atoms in your body experience stress.

Stress is the result of thinking that you are separate and alone.

You may sometimes forget that you have legions of angels working with you on the other side.

Stress requires vast amounts of energy and is never satisfied.

Stress feeds on itself in an endless cycle of expanding and contracting tension.

The antidote to stress is trust.

Trust loosens the tightness in your heart and allows the energy to flow freely.

Trust aligns your energies with universal, divine energies.

Trust allows the knots of tension to unravel in a natural, simple way.

Trust dissolves the fear that created the tension in the first place.

As you remember to trust, you are relieved of fear and the tightness in your heart vanishes.

Notice the difference in your life when you trust.

Think how much different your life would be if you could live in a state of trust *every single moment*.

The miracles are just *the beginning!*

Trust.

Cultivate Your Light

The way to endure the dark of winter is to cultivate the light in your heart.

Winter will always have its darkness.

You must make sure that you always have *your light*.

The light within can never be extinguished, but you may forget this when darkness overtakes you.

As you cultivate your inner light, you cultivate a way of seeing, even through the deepest black.

Your light shines beyond you and lights the way for others, too.

Even the tiniest light is a beacon in the darkness.

Cultivate your inner light and the outer darkness has no power to engulf you.

Darkness and light have their own cycles.

As you become lighter on the inside, you lengthen its cycle and the darkness becomes shorter.

There will always be darkness in this realm, just as there will always be winter.

This is the realm of contrast.

You must *go through* the darkness.

Sometimes it may seem as if there is no inner light .

That's when you must remember the cycles: The cycle of the outer seasons, and the cycle of the inner seasons.

Focus your energy on your inner light and it will grow brighter.

Focus on your inner light and the darkness cannot overtake you.

ᕦ᎐ ᕦ᎐ ᕦ᎐

Change Fear into Excitement!

When you want to try something new and you become fearful, change that fear into *excitement!*

Catch the fear when it's just starting to emerge.

At this point there is little difference between what the mind perceives as fear and what the mind perceives as excitement, so it's easier to change.

Fear is debilitating.

Excitement is liberating.

Become aware so that you can stop the mind from its downward spiral into fear and bring it into the uplifting freedom of excitement.

Any new venture can be derailed by fear if you let it.

Any new venture can be fed by excitement if you transform the fear.

Feel the excitement as it fills every cell in your body with energy.

Think about how good you feel as you begin your new venture.

See yourself achieving your dreams!

Let the power of success flow through your being.

Feel it, see it, taste it, and hear it.

Know on a deep, inner level that the excitement is necessary in order for you to achieve your goals.

Thank it for being in your life.

Allow it to flourish and provide the energy to accomplish your dreams.

Fear doesn't have a chance when you transform it into excitement!

Disempowering the Voice of Fear

The critical mind is the voice of fear.

Fear may speak to you constantly, seeking to extinguish the light of love.

You disempower that critical voice by noticing it, and becoming aware that it is *not you*.

The only power the critical mind has is the attention *you give it*.

Fear thrives on the energy you provide it with your attention!

Your attention is its *only* energy source.

If you *try to stop* your critical mind, you give it power, because *trying* is actively engaging it.

Do the opposite of trying.

Let go, and fear is cut off from its power source.

Fear cannot exist *without you*.

Your attention is its sole source of power.

Fear cannot exist in the open arms of love.

The critical mind is *not you*, just as hatred and resentment are not you.

The critical mind *cannot* be you or you couldn't be aware of it.

Whatever you are aware of is not you!

You become stronger by being aware in each moment.

Become aware of what your critical mind is saying.

Become aware that the critical mind is fear.

Put your energies in the power of love.

Live in love and be *free of fear*.

Live in love and disempower the voice of fear.

Your Vehicle for Creation

Do you use your body, or does it use you?

Do you use your mind, or does it use you?

Do you use your emotions, or do they use you?

Does your body use you to feed it extra food so that it numbs itself?

Does your mind keep you in a constant state of worry and chaos?

Do your emotions keep you in a constant cycle of extremes?

Who are you, who is controlled by these things?

Who are you, if you are *not* these things?

If you are not in control of your body, your mind, and your emotions, who or what is?

If you were in control of them, how would you have them be?

What would it *feel* like to manage your energies?

The first step in managing your energies is becoming aware that they are *not you.*

Learning to manage your energies is the *first step* in spiritual evolvement.

Think of your body, your mind and your feelings as vehicles to get you from one place to another.

Where do you want to go and how do you want your journey to be?

The paradox is that the more you realize the body, the mind, and the emotions are not you, the less control you *need.*

The less control you need, the more energy you have to use your body, your mind, and feelings to create, which is why you have them in the first place!

∾ ∾ ∾

True Success

The essence of life is love.

Measure the success of your life not in terms of material treasures, but in terms of the love you have given to others.

Of course, love cannot truly be measured.

Love can only be lived.

The more you tap into that internal stillness of love, the more you can express it in your daily life.

You have an endless source of pure love within.

No one has a greater or lesser amount.

It has no quantity, but exists in the infinite realm of the non-physical.

This endless source of love is the most powerful energy in the universe.

The power of love creates life itself!

It is personal and impersonal at the same time.

Once you tap into this power, you truly understand that every soul is worthy of love.

When you experience this deep, internal vortex of energy, individual identities become lovable, regardless of their external nature.

There is no one from whom you could withhold this love!

Its natural flow is to everyone and everything.

You, as an individual soul, become a point, a place, from which this love flows to all others.

You become a person from which love - and life - flows.

You become an incredible blessing to others, and immeasurable blessings naturally return to you.

How much greater a success can one be?

༄ ༄ ༄

The Realms of Awe

Experience the wonders of being in this earthly realm.

The sun glistening through the gossamer of a dragonfly's wing.

The smoothness of chocolate in your mouth.

The slight sting of the ocean's spray as you walk along a sandy beach.

The smell of a new puppy's tummy.

The sound of rain drops pattering on dry leaves.

The irrepressible joy of shared love.

These wonders elevate you into the realms of awe, vast beyond perception.

As you allow yourself to be elevated beyond your perceptions, you experience the expanded states of consciousness that unify you with *all that is.*

These expanded states include material *and* non-material realms.

These expanded states allow you to become one with the very forces of life and creativity.

In these pure states you can see the perfection in all.

At these levels you know there is no need for transformation, because everything is perfect the way it is.

This is the holy perspective of being one with all.

Begin cultivating appreciation for the wonders in the earthly realm and you will be led to the glories in the next.

෨ ෨ ෨

Choosing Your Life

You have the ability to *begin your life* all over again, at *each single moment.*

Each single moment can be the beginning of an entirely new world as you become aware of your creative energies in the present.

If something happens to disrupt who you are - if you become angry, distracted, or resentful - simply make the decision to start all over again in this moment.

Don't let others' conception of time determine your life.

Your life is happening *now,* in this instant.

Make a decision, in this moment, about how you *want* to feel.

Decide, just for now, what emotion you want to experience.

Do you want to feel tranquil, at peace, with unlimited creativity flowing from you?

Do you want to feel agitated, upset, and stuck in the grips of worry?

Until you realize you have a choice *each instant* to create your experience of life, you will not choose.

Not choosing is a choice.

What are you choosing?

Don't forget - if you're not happy with your choices, you can *change your mind.*

Be who you want to be in this moment, and this moment becomes your past.

Be who you want to be in this moment and you never have to worry about your future.

∾ ∾ ∾

The Parts of You That You Don't Know

Your unconscious mind is functioning at full throttle all the time.

It is always on the go.

As you become aware in the present moment, you become aware of what is going on in your unconscious mind.

There is nothing unholy about your unconscious mind.

There is no reason to fear it.

Your fear may be a result of thinking that the "real" you is some awful creature who must be kept hidden at all times.

Actually, the real you is more holy than the most holy presence you can imagine.

The real you is more beautiful than anything you have seen.

The real you is glorious, peaceful, and utterly free.

Fear is a result of the ego's thinking.

You are not your thinking.

Thinking is a result of electrical impulses.

Who you really are is far greater than these electrical impulses.

Who you really are is what is *aware* of the electrical impulses in the physical realm.

As you learn to be aware of the impulses, you learn to control them.

This happens by being *aware* in this moment.

This awareness allows the unconscious mind to experience peace.

Be aware, be still, experience peace, and honor the unconscious mind for all the work it is doing for you.

Don't Resist – Persist!

Negative thinking is simply the result of conditioning.

It's not just your thinking that gets conditioned; your body and your emotions do as well.

Your thinking sets up an emotional response, which in turn affects the body.

It's impossible to have a thought without affecting the emotions.

It's impossible to have an emotion without affecting the body.

Therefore, thoughts affect *every aspect* of your being.

That is why it is so important to direct your thinking in a positive, uplifting direction.

You can only direct your thinking as you become aware of your thoughts in the present moment.

The first step is to be aware of what you're thinking.

Don't resist what emerges.

Remember, "What you resist, persists."

Don't *resist*; *persist* in being aware.

Thoughts have only the power you give them.

Think about it: A thought is just a thought unless you give it energy by focusing on it.

As you give your thoughts attention, they become more powerful.

The more attention you give negative thoughts, the more you condition yourself to think them.

Bring your attention into the moment and you condition yourself to let negative thoughts go so you can focus on the positive.

Your Most Important Words

The words you speak to yourself are the most important ones you say.

They set the foundation for everything else you do.

Everything you do on the outside *begins* on the inside.

If you aren't speaking to yourself in a positive manner, then you cannot be a positive influence in the world.

How you speak reflects how you think.

If your speaking isn't clear, your thinking isn't clear.

If your thinking isn't clear, your energies are muddled and difficult to manage.

Speaking to yourself is simply a reflection of how your internal energies are aligned.

Become aware of your inner voice.

Is it *your* voice?

If it's not your voice, whose voice is it?

What is its primary message?

If it's not your voice and it's not giving you positive messages, change it into a silly, helpless, cartoon character's voice, so it doesn't have any power over you.

Now cultivate *your inner voice.*

Give it a sound that is soothing, loving, strong, and positive.

Give your inner voice all the qualities that will help your soul unfold into the beautiful being you are.

Speak softly and speak wisely.

How you speak to yourself determines your life!

Death is Only the Body's End

Why is death feared?

Is it because death is thought of as the end?

You may think of death as the end because the body disintegrates and returns to the earth.

You may think of death as the end because you identify with the body.

When you identify with the body you naturally experience fear.

The body is a temporary vehicle that exists in a relative realm - it has a beginning, a middle, and an end.

The more you identify with the body, the more you will suffer.

The more you identify with the body, the greater your fear of death.

The more aware you become that you are a spiritual being temporarily occupying a human body, the less you experience fear and all other negative emotions.

The more aware *you become* in your body, the more you realize death is not an end, but an opportunity to experience other realms in other ways.

Fear becomes a faint shadow, no longer able to grip your heart.

Death has no power over you because you don't give it the energy of fear.

Death is the body's end, *not the soul's!*

What Are You Waiting For?

Don't wait until you are inspired to begin your work.

Begin your work and inspiration will follow.

It is up to you to take the first step, to paint the first stroke, to write the first word, to play the first note.

Once you begin, the energy of the entire universe is there to help you.

If you wait, you put yourself in a state of fear.

By making the first move you enter into the energy of this moment, where creativity and energy flow naturally.

There is no prerequisite for creativity.

There is no prerequisite for living fully in this moment.

Begin *now*.

Make the decision to use your energies to begin whatever project you have in mind.

It could be planting a flower.

It could be emptying the garbage.

It could be writing a poem.

Begin and become aware of the energy that naturally flows through you.

Then just keep beginning!

Don't think about what you have accomplished or what you will accomplish.

Just keep beginning.

Thank your angels for assisting you.

Glory in being an instrument of divine energy.

Notice how good it feels as the creativity seems to take on a life of its own.

Your responsibility is *to begin* and allow the forces of creation to do the work.

What are you waiting for?

Your Soul (Sole) Need

You are here on this planet to love.

Everything else is a waste of time.

As you begin to let love be the motivation for everything you do, your entire body becomes holy.

Your needs diminish as you discover your sole (soul) need: To love.

As you look through the eyes of love, everything in your life evolves to a higher vibration.

The love you see through your new eyes is contagious.

The love you feel in your heart is felt in the hearts of others.

The need to defend is gone, thus the need to attack is gone as well.

Love needs no defense.

Love is at the deepest core of your being.

Underneath the resistance, underneath the hiding, underneath all the layers of doubt, negativity and fear, is a core of infinite love.

As you learn to trust that this love is *who you really are,* your channels of energy clear, and you become a vehicle for even more love.

Your holy nature emerges and lights the way for those around you, so that the love multiplies, expands, and spreads throughout the entire globe.

Your light becomes an affirmation of light in others and helps their inner core of love to emerge.

Love.

Don't waste your time.

Be a light of love and fulfill your earthy mission.

There is No Hierarchy Among Humans

One measure of your maturity is how you treat people you consider "beneath" you.

Regardless of your social standing, there are those in your life who you may deem inferior in some way.

What is it that makes you superior?

The belief that you are superior to others inherently implies the belief that you are also inferior to others.

How do you treat people you believe are inferior?

What is it about you that is superior?

What if no rank existed among humans?

How would that realization change your life?

Didn't Jesus mingle with prostitutes?

Didn't He refuse to argue with Pontius Pilate?

What do you think He knew about people that allowed Him to function with such grace?

Did He feel superior to prostitutes?

How do you think they would have responded to Him if He did?

Did He feel inferior to Pontius Pilate?

How do you think Pontius Pilate would've treated Jesus if He had felt inferior?

Perhaps Jesus didn't judge others.

Perhaps He didn't judge himself.

Perhaps Jesus didn't have the *need* to evaluate himself using human standards.

How would *your* life be different if you were able to give up judgment?

Perhaps giving up judgment is what opens the door to unconditional love.

What "higher" form of maturity is there?

Is Everyone God?

Just for a moment, believe that everyone is God.

Decide that everyone you encounter today is God.

What divine attributes would you give these people?

Would they become kind, loving, compassionate, and nonjudgmental?

Or would they become stern, judging, and aloof?

Would you welcome others' divine presence or would you be afraid?

How *you think* about God has a major impact on your entire life.

How you think about *others* has a major impact on your entire life.

The key is deciding *how to think* about both.

You can make the decision to think about God in a way that is beneficial and empowering to you.

Experiment with your thinking until you find a method that works best.

What you believe God is and others are form the core beliefs you hold about *yourself*.

Because these are beliefs, however, you can change them.

Beliefs are merely a conglomeration of thoughts you have adopted.

You might as well change your thoughts so that you can enhance your life.

Experiment.

Decide for today that everyone, *including you*, is God and see what miracles you can create!

The Value of Time and Silence

What is the value of time?

What is the value of silence?

How much time do you give silence in your life?

If you don't value silence, you won't give it time.

There are *two kinds* of silence: external silence and internal silence.

Many people prefer external noise because it distracts them from their internal noise.

Both inner noise and outer noise can monopolize your energy.

Your energies can get so distracted with noise that you aren't able to focus your attention on anything else.

Silence allows you the opportunity to focus.

Time allows you the opportunity to practice.

The better you get at focusing your attention, the better you get at using time.

Time ceases to be an element over which you have no control.

There is no need to control time because it ceases to be an element that has control *over you*.

You become one with the elements; time and silence become vehicles through which you express your energy.

You become a creator of sound rather than being distracted by it.

Silence and time are gifts through which your own individual energies develop and flow.

As you learn to value time, as you learn to value silence, you learn to honor your own divine energy.

It is in the silence that creation takes place, over time.

Divine Guidance

What is divine guidance?

How do you *get it* and how do you know it's *real*?

It would be much easier to accept if it hit you like a bolt of lightening.

That would be something you couldn't dispute.

You must first ask yourself: Do you *want* guidance?

Are you willing to do what you're told?

Are you willing to listen?

There is a difference between wanting your problems solved and being willing to do what is necessary to solve them.

In order to receive guidance you must clear out the mind's debris.

Divine guidance is with you all the time; you just may not recognize it.

It doesn't do you any good to ask for advice and then not listen.

Divine guidance is actually built into your heart, waiting to emerge.

You could not have been born *without* divine guidance.

You will not leave this earth without divine guidance.

Divine guidance is as real as your breath.

Breathe in.

Be still.

Listen.

What is divine guidance telling you now?

∾ ∾ ∾

Tailor the Experience

Think of each experience you've had as a package of energy.

This package contains both positive and negative forces, like a battery.

As you think about the package of a specific experience, think about the negative aspects that you'd like to release.

Now take all the negative aspects out of the package and put them into a beautiful, shimmering sphere.

In your mind's eye, watch as this sphere transports the negativity up into the heavens, up into the hands of God's divine transformation.

And now, take all the *positive forces* in the package and put them into *your heart*.

Experience how good it feels to keep the positive aspects of the experience and let go of the negative.

Sometimes the positive aspects may be difficult to identify.

Sometimes they are hidden and need to be brought into the light.

Become aware of what's in the package after you've removed the negativity.

Maybe a negative experience helped you set boundaries, maybe it helped you learn to love, maybe it showed you another path - the lessons are endless.

From now on, whenever negative energies come up, put them into a sphere and let it rise up so that God can transform them *for you*.

Then remember the lessons you learned and know that those are kept in your heart.

∾ ∾ ∾

Changing Your Inner Voice

What stories does your inner voice tell you?

What tone does it use when it speaks?

Is your inner voice kind and loving?

Many inner voices are harsh, impatient, and mean.

Many people would never use their inner voice with anyone else.

Many are not aware of how cruel their inner voice is or how often it speaks to them.

As you become aware of what your inner voice is saying and how it is saying it, you can take steps to change it into a kind, loving, positive influence in your life.

How would you *like* your inner voice to sound?

How would you *like* to be spoken to?

Think of how your entire life would improve if you changed *just* your inner voice!

Become aware of the comments it makes about other people.

What are you continually telling yourself that is not helpful?

What could your inner voice tell you that would *be* helpful?

You are the *only one* who knows what your inner voice is telling you, and you are the *only one* who can change it.

Begin now.

Become aware of what's being said inside of you.

Change your *inner voice* and your *outer life* will automatically follow.

How Are You Using Your Power?

Imagine that *you* have *created your life.*

Pretend that you chose to have everything in your life as it is right now.

Since you created your life, you can *uncreate* it!

What is it you'd like to change?

How would you make your life different?

How would you make *you* different?

True wisdom knows the difference between what you *can* change and what you *can't.*

As you become more aware, as you become more conscious, you begin to see your role in creating the world around you.

Don't think for one moment that you are powerless.

Believing you are powerless negates your free will.

How are you *using* your power?

What kind of life are you creating?

How are you using your energies?

How would you *like* to use your energies?

What would you like to *be doing* that you're not doing?

What are you doing that you'd like *not* to be doing?

What can you change so that you can have the life you want?

If you can't change it, who can?

If you didn't create your life, who did?

How are you using your power to create your life?

Fear is Your Only Prison

Fear paralyzes with its dark grip on your fragile heart.

You may think you must fight the hand of terror.

Fighting never leads to victory; it only exhausts the body and impairs the soul.

Fighting is the coward's game because its motivation is fear.

True warriors learn to overcome their fear through peace.

Peace is only achieved through stillness.

The same waters that plunge over the waterfall also fill the still pond.

Go into the still pond within and there is no fear.

Fear exists in the realm of the mind.

That's why fighting never overcomes fear, because you cannot fight the mind.

The mind simply *is*.

Fighting the mind is like building a bigger waterfall - the force of turbulence simply increases.

Fighting fear causes more fear.

That's why the way through fear is stillness.

When the mind is quiet, fear has no fuel to exist.

Stillness releases you from the prison of fear.

The quiet of the pond leads to new levels of freedom and wisdom.

Be still.

Stop fighting.

Fear not.

Notice and Focus

What does the expression, "Gather your thoughts," mean?
Where are thoughts that they need to be gathered?
Where do you put them once you have gathered them?

The expressions used in everyday life are important because they truly reflect how you manage your energies.

You must first *identify* your thoughts in order to gather them.

That unsettled feeling you get when you can't "think straight" indicates that your thoughts are scattered and unfocused.

As you learn to become aware of your energies, you naturally become aware of your thinking.

When your thoughts are out of focus, your life is out of focus.

How can you get what you want when you can't manage your thinking?

How can you get what you want in your outer world when you can't get what you want in your inner world?

How do your thoughts serve you in those worlds?

Become aware of what you need to do in order to focus your energies.

Notice and focus, and your energies naturally align.

As your energies align, your thoughts focus.

Notice and focus, and the beauty of the moment becomes the beauty of your life.

Keep in Mind

What is it you'd like to keep in mind?

When you keep something in mind, what is it exactly that you're doing?

Where *is* your mind that you actually keep something in it?

When it's not in your mind, *where is it?*

When you're having trouble in life, it may be that you have negative thoughts you don't know how to change.

Think of your mind as a closet.

There may be clothes in there that don't fit anymore.

There may be items taking up space and preventing you from getting newer, more comfortable items that would suit you better.

There may be old, ragged clothes that you've forgotten you even owned.

In the same way, you must become aware of old, automatic thoughts that run through your mind, so that you can get rid of them.

They may be difficult to detect because they are automatic.

As you become aware of the thoughts you are "keeping in mind," you can decide to let them go, just like you decide to get rid of the old clothes in your closet.

Make the decision to let those old thoughts go so you can make room for new, creative thinking.

Then keep in mind what you are *keeping in mind!*

෨ ෨ ෨

Every Day is an Opportunity

Begin to see every single day as an opportunity for a completely new life.

Every day you can begin your life *all over again*.

What attitudes do you choose to have?

What emotions do you choose to feel?

What memories do you choose to energize?

What kind of person do you choose to be *now*?

You are not stuck with any particular attitude, feeling, memory, or attribute.

You can change the energy you put into any one of these things at any given time, which means that you can change the energy you put into being *who you are* at any given time.

Practice.

Practice being the person you *want* to be.

Begin each day as if it were your birth into this world.

Remember that if you catch yourself behaving or thinking in a way that doesn't fit your ideal, you can make a decision at that moment to change it.

Simply stop.

Become aware of who you want to be.

Now let go of the attitudes that don't fit this ideal.

Practice.

If you forget who you are, simply stop and begin your day all over again.

Your new life begins *now*.

Who do *you* choose to be?

Stop Suffering Now

You must learn to stop suffering now, in this moment.

The idea that you can put up with suffering until some later date is preposterous.

Your body is a gift that allows you to live in time.

Time is the vehicle that prompts you to realize that each moment is holy.

Your physical body is a vehicle that prompts you to realize that each breath is sacred.

As you honor each moment, each breath, you realize you can choose to live in joy *now*.

As you learn to choose joy, suffering automatically stops; it doesn't exist in *this moment*, in *this breath*.

Suffering exists because you don't have your energies aligned in the present moment.

You suffer when you waste the present by projecting your thoughts into the future or the past.

What could be more magical than the energy of this moment?

You live in a body that allows your soul to have form and move through the infinite potential of consciousness!

You are able to use this body to create and put into physical forms your own personal ideas and energy.

Why would you suffer when there is so much joy you can experience?

You don't stop suffering at some magical point in the future; you stop suffering when you learn to live in the magic of each moment.

What if You Didn't Have an Opinion?

You may equate having an opinion with strength, force, and leadership, but in actuality, having an opinion may be simply an effort to prove yourself *right*.

Being right is an attempt to justify your existence.

You may feel uncomfortable not having an opinion because you are so used to justifying.

Being right helps you think you have an important purpose.

When your identity is tied to being right, then being *wrong* is absolutely crushing.

Living in this duality, then, causes you to constantly swing back and forth between elation and devastation.

What if you decided not to have an opinion?

Does it feel like you're giving up your strength when you go to that neutral place?

Who you *really are* cannot be right or wrong.

Who you really are exists in the realm of no judgment.

Come to that place of discovery within, where your soul exists.

Give up the need to be right and join your forces with divine energies.

The ego's strength is minuscule anyway.

Give up the need to be right and get acquainted with who you really are; a beautiful soul in an infinite universe.

To Be Brave

What does it mean to be brave?

To be brave you have to walk through fear.

Bravery is feeling fear and going forward anyway.

If you didn't experience the fear, you *couldn't* be brave!

Your job is not to avoid fear, but to learn to walk through it.

When you don't do something because you're afraid, it's like stepping backwards instead of stepping forward.

Of what is it that you're most afraid?

It's important to become aware of your fears, so that they don't exert unconscious control over you.

Once you are conscious of your fears, they've lost fifty percent of their power.

In fact, sometimes awareness is all that's needed to alleviate a fear.

It's when you *resist* fear that it grows stronger.

The harder you try *not* to be afraid, the more fearful you are.

What are you afraid of?

Become aware of the power you're giving fear.

Notice the strength you feel pulling back into yourself when you look at what frightens you.

When you resist, you shut down your internal power supply.

The very nature of resisting causes an internal shutdown.

The greater your honesty in acknowledging your fears, the easier it is to be brave.

What Blessings Can You Give?

Ask every single day, *What blessings can I give the earth?*

Ask every single day, *What blessing can I be to others?*

As you begin to see yourself as a source of blessings, the entire focus of your life will change.

How many blessings are within you to bestow?

The holiness within you is as infinite as the grains of sand along the shore.

Within you are gifts beyond what the tiny, human mind can imagine.

Within you is the power to create a smile or a tear.

Within you is the power to create laughter or fear.

How do you choose to grace God's world?

Do you choose to be a blessing or a curse?

The energy you send out multiplies and comes back to bless or curse you a thousandfold.

As you send blessings, you receive them.

The more you focus on what you can give, the more *you can give*.

Be a smile and receive a smile.

Be a blessing and receive a blessing.

How do you choose to bless today?

☙ ☙ ☙

Receiving Allows Others the Joy of Giving

How do you *receive* help from others?

How do you receive blessings from this world?

You must be able *to receive* in order *to give.*

Most people think it's the other way around, but that's not so.

If you exercise graciousness in all aspects of your life, then others are allowed the joy of giving.

If no one receives, how can anyone give?

Existing in the human body forces you to live outside of your spiritual comfort zone, requiring you to stretch to new levels of soul maturity.

Some have learned to give and now must learn to receive.

Some have learned to receive and now must learn to give.

You are meant to be here, now, exactly where you are, so that you can bless the world with your energy and receive the energy of the world's blessings.

Giving and receiving are natural cycles of energy, and both must be experienced to achieve balance.

"Ask, and you shall receive."

And, "*Receive, so that others may give!*"

༈ ༈ ༈

Accessing Your Soul's Power

Simply decide *not* to be helpless.

Decide right now to use your power.

Choose to feel good *no matter what.*

If you have to pretend, pretend.

Don't let the negativity of others defeat you.

Your soul has chosen your circumstances because they are uniquely suited to help you grow.

As you begin to honor your soul's choices, you begin to empower yourself.

The only person who can make you a victim is *you.*

Regardless of external circumstances, you have the power to choose your reactions.

Practice.

Practice pulling your energy back into the center of your being and feeling your strength.

You don't *need anger* to feel strong.

You don't *need resistance* to be determined.

You can be strong and determined from an inner place of quiet holiness.

In fact, true strength and determination can only arise from stillness.

Weakness is a temporary state that develops from doubt.

Doubt develops when you forget who you are: A divine spiritual being in full control of your destiny.

Decide at this moment to control your destiny and witness the difference in your life.

Become still and access the true power of your soul.

Remember to Bless

Let your first thought of another be a blessing.

And then, when you can't do it anymore, when you're absolutely blessed out, bless yourself.

When you feel the exhaustion of life overcoming you, it's because you need to be the recipient of your own blessings.

The giver is also the receiver.

There are no gifts you can truly give unless you are capable of receiving them.

You must be able to look in the mirror and smile.

In order to touch the Divine inside another, you must be able to touch the Divine inside of *you!*

The beauty you see outside is a reflection of the beauty you see *inside*.

As you honor the Divine in you, it becomes natural to honor the Divine in others.

Bless yourself, and the blessings naturally flow to others.

So, let the first thought you have of others, like the first thought you have of yourself, be a blessing!

෨ ෨ ෨

The Field of Super-Consciousness

How do you allow your consciousness to shift?

Why would you want your consciousness to shift, anyway?

The value of allowing your consciousness to shift is that it allows *you* to shift.

Shifting your consciousness is equivalent to making a quantum leap in awareness.

It is only through awareness that you become conscious of your choices.

When you have a shift in consciousness, you have access to a whole new set of choices.

Do you want only one shift of consciousness?

Do you want only one new set of choices?

Of course not!

You want as many shifts and as many choices as suit you.

Believing that you have accomplished all by experiencing one shift of consciousness is limiting.

It's like saying you can change your mind only one time.

Learn to live beyond the mind.

Learn to live in the field of infinite choice.

Learn to allow your consciousness to shift at will.

Then it doesn't need to shift because it isn't confined to one dimension.

You then have access to super-consciousness, where all choices exist, where all miracles are created!

Sing Your Song

What melody does your soul sing?

What rhythm does your heart beat?

What harmony do your lungs breathe?

You have a melody, a rhythm, and a harmony that *only you* are attuned to.

When you are in tune with your song, you are not only operating at your optimal personal level, you are also operating at the level at which you can best serve the universe.

You cannot best serve the universe until you best serve yourself.

Ask yourself, "What do I need? What do I want? What pleases me? How do I want to spend my time?"

These questions are not designed to encourage you to be selfish, but to *know* yourself.

You must know yourself to be in tune with your song.

Amazingly, when you are in tune with your own song, you are in *natural harmony with others*.

Sing, breathe, feel your heartbeat; live in the joy of being connected to the harmony of your unique song.

You are the *only one* who can sing your song.

Your song is always with you.

It is a gift from the divine universe.

The more you sing it, the more it returns to you.

Sing in joy.

Love your song.

Know your song so you can know yourself.

A Life With No Limits

Just for a moment, think of what your life would be like if you had no limits.

Become aware of the limits you have now.

Become aware of inner limits and outer limits.

What are the limits you can release and what are the limits you can't release?

Become aware that anger, resentment, remorse, and regret are self-imposed blocks that limit both your inner and your outer energy flows.

These negative emotions limit you because you mistakenly accept them as valid parts of who you are.

As you become aware that these feelings can be released, and you make the decision to release them, you come closer to discovering your true identity, which is naturally free of any limitations.

Your greatest limits are not external, but internal.

If you are free on the inside you can overcome almost anything on the outside.

How do you release the inner knots of hatred, blame and frustration?

Give them to God.

Give the negative knots to your heavenly guides and angels, and let them untie them and release them to God.

Your natural state is free, open, expanding, and unlimited.

Get to know who you really are – without limits!

Start Having Fun!

How do you play?

What do you like to do in your "free" time?

These are important activities to cultivate because they are rejuvenating.

Become aware of the levels of consciousness you experience as you're having fun.

Chances are your thoughts are not centered on yourself when you're having fun.

Chances are your thoughts are not centered on another when you're playing.

Chances are your thoughts are in the moment, centered in the activity that you're enjoying.

That is why you're having fun!

You're having fun because all your energies are congruent.

When you are in joy, your energy systems are balanced.

Notice the lightness you feel when you play.

It actually attracts even more light to you, which is why play is energizing and fun.

As you experience the full impact of being totally present, each moment becomes fun, full of play.

Play is then not limited to a certain activity, but becomes part of all activities because it is realized in each moment.

Live now.

Play now.

Start having fun!

∽ ∽ ∽

True Freedom

What if life had no rules?
What if you had no restrictions?
What if you had complete control over your energies?
Isn't that what freedom is?

Isn't freedom the ability to choose how to use your energies?

When you develop the skills necessary to utilize your energies as you wish, you create your own rules - you are truly free.

It may seem like a paradox that in order to become free you must develop skills, but it is in the development of discipline that true freedom lies.

It is only through discipline, through practice, that you learn to harness and direct your energies.

True freedom lies not in being out of control; true freedom lies in being *in control*.

True freedom lies not in the ability to be in control of others, but to be in *control of self*.

When you are out of control, you are *choosing chaos*, which is the same as giving your power to something outside of yourself.

As you learn to choose from the center of your being, your God-self, you naturally follow Divine rules.

True freedom is being in alignment with your God-self, allowing Divine energy to choose for you.

✑ ✑ ✑

True Resurrection

Every person has the opportunity to experience resurrection.

Your true self is resurrected after the ego has been crucified.

The ego is that part of you that wants to be right, that defends your life.

Your true life, however, *begins* when you connect with your soul-self: Who you really are on a deep, inner level.

That is your resurrection.

That is when you become an open channel through which God's holy light shines.

It is the ego within that hates.

It is the ego that is wounded.

It is the ego that wants revenge.

Who you really are cannot hate, cannot be wounded, and cannot take revenge.

It is your *need to love* that propels you through the universe!

Your desire to be a conduit of divine love is the evolutionary force that ultimately guides your life.

Your ego isn't evil; it simply isn't motivated by love.

That's why it has to be crucified.

The ego has to use all its energy before it gives up.

You know you are coming from a holy place when you are coming from love.

That is when you are truly resurrected.

Surrender the ego to divine love and allow yourself to experience resurrection.

That's when your true life begins.

❦ ❦ ❦

How to Get Out of a Bad Mood

Many times when you are in a "bad mood" it's because you've created an imaginary scenario in the future, and then react to it as if it were happening *now*.

The bad mood results when you create a scenario that impacts you in a negative way.

This is an example of how not living in the present moment impacts your life.

Any time you put your energies into the future or the past, you're zapping your life force in the present.

You may think you want to escape the present, but escape only causes delay.

Delays simply cause regret over the past.

As you focus your energies in the present, you naturally create a future and therefore a past, over which you have no regrets.

Focus on the present, and your bad mood will be a thing of the past!

ॐ ॐ ॐ

Catch Your Thoughts

If you don't "catch" your thinking, you won't have the opportunity to become aware of who you really are.

Your thinking becomes your master, unless you master it.

How do you "catch" a thought?

Simply become aware in the moment of what you are thinking.

At times, you can't distinguish between who you are and what your thoughts are.

That's when your thoughts have control over you.

When you are that identified with your thoughts, you become their slave.

At that point, your thoughts are in control and you are not exercising your divine free will.

You have lost awareness of who you really are and your identity has been submerged.

You don't "think" you're in control because your *thinking* is in control.

When this happens, you live like a zombie, and the extreme pity is that you don't even know it!

"Control" has been given a bad name only because most people don't have it.

The irony is that the way you achieve control is to become aware of your thoughts.

The price of awareness is "paying" attention.

Simply notice your thoughts.

Become aware that they are *not you*.

"Catch" your thinking and become aware of *who you are*.

The Mysteries of the Universe

The treasures of the universe are within you.

The essence of your soul is the center of creation.

As you learn to tap into this marvelous center, you learn to create heaven on earth.

When you accept that you are a mystical being, you open the doors into the realms of miracles.

Part of the resistance to this process is fear that you will lose your individuality and become immersed in the undifferentiated universe.

This fear is in your mind, which is why you can't use the mind to get to the essence of who you really are.

Events of the mind keep you from accessing the elements of the soul.

Doubt does not exist at the soul level.

That's why you must go beyond "thinking" to know who you really are.

When you come to know who you are, what you do with that knowledge will naturally emerge.

Even though you have no limits, you are distinctly individual and unique.

Truth always has an element of paradox.

As you go within and find your own treasures, you become eminently more aware of the treasures in others.

Take joy in your own presence, and the joy you take in others will multiply.

This is the greatest treasure of all: Discovering the mysteries of the universe!

Your Holy Soul is Without Blemish

Your deepest secrets cannot destroy you.

The surest way to let go of the anguish of your inner fears is to share you darkest secrets with someone you trust.

Secrets only have the power you give them.

Your dark secrets are inner judgments against yourself.

Those inner judgments create a false guilt that makes you fear exposing your innermost self.

The irony is that what you fear exposing *isn't you* at all!

What you fear exposing is a false sense of self that believes *it is the negativity* within that requires hiding!

It is afraid because it isn't real.

Who you really are is never afraid!

Who you really are can never be hurt or experience anguish.

Who you really are doesn't have secrets.

As you begin to identify with your true nature rather than your false nature, you begin to let go of the blocks that keep you tied to the false self.

Don't hide behind the secrets of the false self.

Be who you really are: Holy, free, loving, infinite, and indestructible.

Letting Go of Confusion

Confusion is a distraction of the ego.

It needs confusion to justify its existence.

Confusion gives the ego a job - the job of figuring out things.

As long as the ego, the linear mind, has something to do, it feels justified in existing.

That's why the linear mind can't be still.

The ego equates stillness with death.

The ego thinks it's fighting for its life when you try to achieve stillness in meditation.

That's why "trying" doesn't work.

"Trying" occurs at the ego level, not the soul level.

The ego loves to "try" - that's its function.

The ego can't experience stillness because stillness doesn't occur at the ego-level of consciousness.

When you live solely in ego-level consciousness, your life is filled with confusion.

You learn to rise above the ego by *letting it go*.

Resisting the linear mind simply gives it more power.

The ego loves a good fight, which gives it more energy.

In order to use the ego instead of the ego using you, give it to God.

Give the struggles, the fighting, and the manipulating to divine will, so that you can enjoy the peace that is your destiny.

Give the ego's confusion to God - it's not really yours anyway.

Do Not Defend Yourself

Unless you are in a court of law, there is no need to defend yourself.

The very act of defending yourself puts you in a state of war.

When you catch yourself being defensive, ask, "Who am I fighting, and why?"

You may be surprised to discover how often you engage in warfare.

As you succumb to the *game* of defense, you automatically fall into the *trap* of offense.

Simply ask yourself if you want to fight.

There is freedom in *not* fighting.

When you give up fighting you rise above the rules of warfare.

What greater freedom is there than that?

You can't be who you really are as long as you're involved in a game.

There is no true freedom as long as you're living your life responding to the rules of a game.

Responding defensively or offensively implies a lack of freedom, because both responses are confining.

Choose *not* to justify yourself, and you choose freedom.

Let the courts of law handle defense.

Let Peace Come to You

Quality of life and peace of mind are synonymous.

It doesn't matter how high a quality of life you have unless you have peace mind.

Riches mean nothing if you have inner turmoil.

Your natural state is calm, centered, and clear.

Who you truly are experiences no turmoil.

Who you truly are exists in a place of endless peace.

The secret to living a life of peace is to remember *who you really are.*

When you identify with your body, your emotions, or your thoughts, you doom yourself to a life of destruction.

Don't identify – *be.*

Identification is a process of the mind.

You cannot discover who you are through thinking.

The path to enlightenment does not exist in the mind.

The mind is here to serve you; you are not here to serve it.

If you exist in any state except peace, you are your mind's servant.

Don't try to control the mind.

Simply become aware of how it is using *your energy.*

The mind exists in a state of its own.

Don't try to achieve peace.

Just *be*, and peace will come to you.

Be a Vehicle for God's Energy

A certain amount of detachment is required in order for the Holy Spirit to work through you.

If there is too much emotion, too much "wanting," too much desire, then there is no room for divine light to enter.

It helps to develop detachment - to be able to view the outcome without concern.

The outcome is really not your responsibility anyway.

You are a vehicle through which God's energy works.

You, personally, can't know what the outcome is supposed to be on a cosmic level.

You must rise above the level of appearances to be effective.

If you allow what appears to be true affect your actions, you will always be stuck at the linear-level mind.

Detachment does not mean not caring.

Detachment means caring enough not to get involved on a personal, ego level.

Detachment means clearing yourself of emotional debris so that divine energy can work through you.

You don't need to concern yourself with the outcome when you are aligned with sacred love.

Be determined to be a channel for God's will, yet detached from the *apparent* outcome.

Delight in Yourself

The delights in life are truly simple.

There is no greater delight than knowing you are loved.

There is no greater gift you can give another than sharing with them that *they* are loved.

This gift, this experience of being loved, is not based on intellect.

This is a deep, inner knowing upon which all other esoteric knowledge is based.

Who is it that loves?

This inner love, by definition, does not emanate from outside of you.

Paradoxically, this deep, inner self-love is not personal.

It's not personal because it does not exist on the ego-level.

Self-love on the ego level is not love; it's self-absorption.

Once this inner love is recognized, it explodes into the outer realms and encompasses all that is.

At first it seems exquisitely one-pointed, personal and unique, and then it becomes expansive, all encompassing, and universal.

This self-love is what fills the emptiness within and creates universes from the black holes in the abyss.

Begin delighting in yourself, and watch your inner treasures emerge.

Such simple love creates entire universes!

∾ ∾ ∾

Ego Heaven/Ego Hell

Placing oneself either above or below another is simply the ego's attempt to be "right."

Being "right" in the ego's mind is enslaving because you then live in fear of being wrong.

Being wrong is hell for the ego.

The ego's very existence is a struggle to always be right, always be "better than," always be in control.

Ego heaven can never be experienced because it's a goal that's always in the future, never in the here and now.

The ego's very existence depends upon creating strife.

Your highest good is served not when you try to destroy the ego, but when you *rise above it*.

You serve your highest good when you recognize the ego, and then choose to be who you are on a *soul level*: Strong, holy, loving, in this very moment.

You achieve this state when you remember who you are, when you give up the false identity of ego-hell, and when you recognize that the same inner holiness that exists within you exists in all others.

This state of being is not achieved; it is lived, moment-by-moment, second-by-second.

You do not need to believe that you are better or worse than anyone else, because we are all human, all one, all holy.

❧ ❧ ❧

Criticism's Curse

Criticism does not discriminate; criticism curses.

Criticism curses twice: It curses both the giver and the receiver.

When you give criticism it lowers your own vibrations; it lowers your vibrations when you accept it as well.

You may experience a fleeting surge of energy when you criticize, but it's negative energy.

You undoubtedly know the "ego-deflation" associated with receiving criticism.

You must learn to be neither a giver, nor a receiver, of this harsh energy.

If you want others to change their behavior, bless them.

As a giver of blessings, you are also a receiver of them.

You do not need to accept criticism from another.

As a conscious being, you can always *choose* what to accept or reject.

Criticism is the destroyer.

Praise is the builder.

Your job is to give what *you want* to receive, and accept only what you want *to give*.

Remember, as you give to others, you give to yourself.

Choose to be a blessing and not a curse, to others as well as yourself.

Each Moment is Magic!

Each moment is propelled by the infinite power of the universe, bursting with the potential that only you can live.

There is no greater power than that which exists right here, right now, in this instant.

Think of it!

This moment in time is bursting with the finest expression of the heavens.

The breath you are taking right now can never be inhaled again.

What you are experiencing right now is not the same as any other experience you have ever had, or will ever have again.

What you are experiencing in this moment is different from what anyone else has ever, or ever will experience!

As you begin to appreciate the magic of each moment, your whole life becomes filled with joy.

As your appreciation grows, you become not only a participant in the flow of divine energy, but co-creator and vessel of that divine energy as well.

The joy you feel is contagious, and spreads as easily as a smile.

As you breathe in joy, it sends a message to every atom in your being that everything is optimal, right here, right now, in the unparalleled magic of this moment.

There is no greater consciousness than the awareness of this eternal, yet never-to-be-lived-again, moment.

Be *aware* of this moment and live in joy.

Wake Up During Your Dreams

Pay attention to your dreams.

Dreams are visions through which mystical information can reach you.

Dreams are vehicles in which your soul travels.

Divine information, inspiration and explanation can occur during dreams.

Dreams are times when the linear, ego-mind is at rest, so that the holographic, mystical realms can be explored.

In dreams the nightmare of ordinary reality ceases, and the extraordinary realms of life become manifest.

Solutions to problems, answers to puzzles, and insights into people can be achieved in your dream state.

Dreams are important because they reflect a side of you not readily available in your waking state.

You can learn to remember your dreams just as you can forget ordinary reality.

Decide what is useful to you.

Is it useful to remember the mystical information you receive in dreams?

Is it useful to forget the negativity associated with certain events in ordinary reality?

The first step in being able to make conscious choices is to become aware at *all levels* of consciousness.

Begin with your dreams.

Wake up during your dreams!

There's absolutely no point in being asleep while you're dreaming!

From Murder to Miracles

Sometimes just a smile is enough to save a life.

An ounce of love has enough energy to change the course of a person's life from murder to miracles.

You never know when *you* may be the channel of that ounce of love!

The mysteries of the universe can unfold with a single glance.

Time has no meaning in the face of enlightenment, so slow down, take a deep breath, and let the light shine through *you*.

As the light shines through you, you become filled with smiles that dissipate fear, anger, and hostility.

You become a blessing to others in ways that you cannot fathom.

And sometimes, the smile that you give away becomes most important to you!

As you become a blessing to yourself, you become a true vehicle of enlightenment for others.

Smiles send waves of light from the heavens, through you, to others, and then back to you again in endless cycles of love.

Smile.

Let the light of love shine through you.

You never know whose life you'll save.

ᖴᖴᖴ

Don't Let Worry Drain Your Soul

Worry drains the soul.

Worry spins vicious threads that keep you caught in a web of insanity.

Worry creates a cocoon of fear that encompasses you with steel strings.

Sometimes you can burst through this cocoon of worry quickly; other times you must emerge slowly, allowing the new energy of faith to caress you gently.

It is important to recognize that worry is a trap from which you *can* free yourself.

You free yourself from worry *one thought at a time.*

If worry were productive, people would be *taught* how to do it!

Simply "catch" your thoughts as they begin the downward spiral of negativity.

Become aware of what your thoughts are doing.

It seems as if they have a mind of their own, doesn't it?

Surely you wouldn't *choose* to send your energies into a bottomless pit of agony!

When you catch your thoughts spiraling down, bring them back to the light of the here and now.

It's a process.

Become aware of what your mind is thinking.

If it's negative at all, bring your energies back into the present moment.

The more you practice, the easier it becomes.

Don't let worry drain your soul.

Practice the art of being free from worry, one thought at a time.

Pet Lessons

Pets allow you to express yourself through multiple avenues of love.

Some people can *only* love freely through their pets.

Pets offer a vehicle through which you can learn unconditional love.

You learn this because of their unconditional love for *you!*

Animals have strengths most humans can only dream of achieving.

Pets offer the magic of their affection and devotion regardless of how they are treated.

Your animal friends give you loyalty seldom matched in the human realm.

Pets help you connect to the earth and connect to the energy of your own heart.

Each animal species is a different form of divine love.

As you recognize divine love in these different forms, you begin to appreciate the various patterns that operate within the human species.

Pets teach you to love freely, with every aspect of your being.

Pets teach how to love without limits!

What greater lesson can you learn than that?

Becoming Time's Master

It's not that you don't have *enough* time, it's that you don't focus your attention in *present* time.

As you learn to keep your attention in the here-and-now, you find that time actually *expands* to accommodate your needs.

You may think of time as being fixed, but it's actually flexible.

You flex time as you learn to focus your attention.

Most people have no idea where their thoughts are at any given moment.

Most people live in a morass of scattered, unfocused energy.

If you can think of time as being an element of your *own thoughts*, it will give you a great advantage in manifesting your intentions.

Isn't it interesting that people think of time as a place?

How *far back* into the past does your memory go?

How *far into* the future do you dare to think?

How much time is wasted by not being in the present?

As you learn to be in the present, time expands.

As you learn to focus in the present, time becomes a moot point (pun intended).

Learn to be time's master, not time's slave.

The Essence of Divine Love ~You!

There is no such thing as being loved too much.
True adoration does not lead to annoyance or conceit.
It leads to humility and grace.
The reality is: *You are truly adored.*
You are loved beyond measure.
Your job is to tap into this love, to realize its power, and to spread its eternal light.
As you tap into this inner force, you feel the foundation of your very essence.
Your *true nature* is the essence of divine love.
Regardless of your past, you have the capacity to express this divine, inner core.
You may be afraid to delve inward because you believe your inner self is less than good.
What a fabulous surprise awaits you when you finally begin your inner journey!
How much energy is wasted trying to cover up your imagined evil?
Let go of the dishonor of your imaginary thinking and align yourself with the natural flow of love.
There is *no value* in the thought that who you really are is evil.
Let go of that thought and allow yourself to bask in the true, everlasting energy of creation: The energy of love.

The Ecstasy of Your Soul

Try to count the joys in your life.

You can't!

Every second of your life is filled with joy, if you only allow yourself to experience it.

The tiniest drop of water contains the joy of the ever-expanding universe!

Each glint of light endlessly laughs off each surface it touches.

Every nerve pathway in your body has the exquisite ability to feel orgasms of delight!

You cannot count the joys in life because they are infinite!

The glory of divine ecstasy lives in each atom, each thought, each ounce of what you might consider "empty" space.

There is no place, no thought, no time where infinite joy cannot be!

It is here, now, in each word you read, in each breath you breathe!

You cannot count the joy because it is not separate; it is not apart from you!

Let the ecstasy of your soul grow into the divine flower of what you came here to be: An individual, exquisite, manifestation of eternal joy!

The Menace of Fear

Fear is the one true menace in life.

Fear is not to be fought; it is to be recognized.

When you simply recognize fear and say to yourself, "Oh, that's fear," you are acknowledging it without giving it strength.

Fear has no power except the power *you give it*.

Fear gives birth to anger, hatred, jealousy, and betrayal.

When you find yourself experiencing any of these emotions, the question to ask yourself is, "What am I afraid of?"

Once you recognize fear, you can make the conscious decision to surrender it to divine energy for transformation.

The best way to appreciate the full impact of fear is to experience its *absence*.

Imagine what your life would be *without* fear.

Feel the freedom of being aligned with divine energy.

When you recognize fear again, make the choice to give it to God.

Feel the freedom of release, feel the relief of letting go.

This is your natural state: Pure, clear, holy, and aligned with God.

As you become more aware, it becomes easier to give fear to God and live in the endless, creative flow of divine love.

The Miracle of Surrender

At the heart of every great tradition, religion, and philosophy is surrender to God.

Your first thought of surrender may be to *give up,* as if you had lost a battle.

True surrender is not resignation.

True surrender is assignation.

True surrender results when you lovingly and willingly assign your life to God.

As you offer yourself to the Divine, to be used in Its holy way, your life takes on a whole new essence.

In a sense, you are giving up a fight: the fight with your ego.

You're giving up the need to be right.

You're giving up the need to be afraid.

You're giving up the fear of losing.

When you give up the internal fight, you can give up the external fight.

Surrendering to the Divine is the most powerful decision you can make.

When you align your energy with this holy power, miracles happen!

Surrender to the Divine and watch the miracles unfold!

Honor the Light, Not the Darkness

Fear is not to be honored; it is to be overcome.

You honor fear when you don't do something that you want to because you're afraid.

When you act *in spite* of fear, you honor the holiness within.

As you honor your own, inner truth, fear diminishes.

Fear lives on the power you give it.

Fear can't live when you withdraw your energy from it.

Fear can be like a shadow in the night, or a screaming phantom in your face.

If fear stares at you, stare back.

Hold your space in love and light.

Honor the love and the light within and fear has no place to enter.

You may have to go far down the road of fear before you realize that all you need to do is light a small candle, and the darkness of fear is gone.

It is not *what* you are afraid of that hurts you; it is the fear itself.

Fear cannot hold onto you when you let it go.

Fear cannot exist in the sacred light of your soul's brightness.

As you honor your holy self, your light shines brighter and brighter, overcoming all obstacles, all fears and all darkness.

Honor the *light* within, not the darkness.

Your Crucial Inner Conversations

The conversations you have with yourself are the most crucial ones you can have, because they determine what you will do in the outer world.

Internal conversations actually determine, to a great extent, your entire life.

Internal conversations are the foundations of your inner life, which is the *foundation* of your outer life.

That's why it is so important to become aware of what you are saying to yourself.

Decide to *choose* what you say to yourself.

As you choose what to say to yourself, you empower yourself.

Your *thoughts* determine how you feel and what actions you take.

How do you change your internal conversations so that your highest good is served?

Say "yes" to the positive thoughts and "no" to the negative thoughts.

As soon as you catch yourself thinking a negative thought, change it immediately to a positive one.

In this way, your entire energy field will lighten.

As you lighten, negativity has a harder time entering your energetic field.

Practice.

Empower yourself with positive inner conversations.

Spend Time With Yourself

There is a difference between spending time *alone* and spending time *with* yourself.

You can be alone and never get to know yourself.

There are so many distractions - T.V., Internet, movies, music, etc., - that in spite of being *by* yourself, you are not *with* yourself.

Being *with* yourself allows the opportunity to become aware of your thinking.

You can't do this if you aren't quiet enough to listen.

As you become quiet, you first hear the chatter of the world.

You hear sounds and noises that are outside of you.

As you become quieter still, you become aware of your *internal* chatter.

You might become aware of a particular song playing in your head.

You might become aware of conversations that took place in the past.

You might become aware of imaginary conversations that you think may take place in the future.

As you become aware of the activity in your mind, you begin to know yourself.

It is what's shaping your life.

It is where your energies are invested.

As you become aware of your inner life, you get to know yourself in a whole new way.

Spend time *with* yourself so that you can *know* yourself.

Space Aliens and Weird Creatures

Let's say there *are* space aliens and weird creatures that live under the earth's crust.

That reality would not change the eternal message of the most powerful force in the universe - love.

Whether there are space creatures or not doesn't change your relationship with yourself, with others (including the creatures, if there are any) and with divine energy.

The same God that watches over you watches over *everything* and *everyone*.

Your capacity to experience other realities and other realms is governed by your capacity to give up judgment and experience acceptance.

As you learn to give up the confines of conventional thinking, you learn to experience the mystical realms.

The walls that rumble metaphorically in the third dimension as you experience other dimensions are still standing when you return.

All realities co-exist.

There is no need to tear down one reality in order to experience another.

The force that wants you to negate other realities is fear.

Fear contracts your energies and keeps you in the third dimension.

Don't fight fear - simply recognize it.

Fighting fear keeps you at its energetic level.

True progress requires letting go of fear.

And if space aliens and underground creatures exist, so what!

That doesn't change the universal law of love, now and forever.

Choose Your Thoughts!

You are making choices every second, whether you are aware of it or not.

You are making a *choice* to read this.

You are reacting internally to what you have just read, and you are choosing how you react to *that reaction!*

You can change your reaction once you become aware of it, but not before.

Unless you become conscious of what's happening inside of you, you can't make the decision to choose what you *want* to be happening inside of you.

You may "think" you have no power to choose your thoughts, and that "thinking" keeps you a victim of them.

Of what thoughts are you aware?

If you are aware of your thoughts, they cannot be you!

You are the one who is aware.

You are the one who chooses.

You choose every moment and those choices determine your life.

They determine how you feel and what actions you take.

The more conscious choices you make, the more power you have.

Your choices influence not only your life, but the lives of those around you.

Choose to choose, and a whole new energy will open up to you.

Peace is an Inside Job

Peace has nothing to do with what's going on *outside* of you.

Wars are created in the hopes that peace can be felt afterwards, but that's an illusion.

Peace can never be felt externally.

Peace has to do with *your* energies being in alignment.

When you are upset or angry or confused or frustrated, your energies are out of alignment.

If you want peace for others, quit trying to change them!

If you want peace for yourself, quit trying to change others!

It all boils down to the same thing: Acceptance.

When you accept yourself and others, you give yourself permission to experience peace.

Just become aware in this moment of what *is*.

Don't judge it.

Judging is the first step away from peace.

As you tap into the peace within, you become aware of what you can change and what you cannot change.

This awareness naturally enhances your inner state of peace.

That's why peace is an inside job!

Breathe in Your Dreams

What are your dreams?
Why are you here?
What do you hope to experience?
Focus on these things.

Put your inner energies into *fulfilling your life's purpose* and everything else will take care of itself.

You are the only one who can fulfill your purpose.

Breathe *in* your dreams!

Breathe *out* your fears.

Breathe *in* your life.

Breathe *out* your hurts.

You are the only one who can breathe in your life and your dreams.

You are the only one who can breathe out your fears and your hurts.

Breathe in joy!

Breathe out anger.

Breathe in happiness!

Breathe out sadness.

Inhale the sweet fragrance of bliss!

Exhale the stale smell of self-pity.

Be who you are: Pure, sweet, divine, holy energy.

Let go of who you are not; angry, afraid and stagnant.

You are the *only one* who can truly experience the exquisite nature of your being.

Let each breath fill you with an internal celebration of who you are!

Breathe in your dreams and give them the energy to manifest.

Growing Through God's Love

Every day spent on this earth is an opportunity to grow.

No matter how feeble or insignificant you *think* you are, the time you spend here is a time for learning and teaching.

Some of the time is designed for you to help others learn, and some is designed for you to learn.

Time is a precious commodity; once spent, it cannot be replaced.

Each moment here is a blessing, an opportunity for you to share God's love with others.

Sometimes this love is shared with a smile, sometimes with a word, sometimes with a touch, sometimes with a thought.

Every way you share God's love is important.

Think of your life as an opportunity to allow God to smile *through* you, to speak *through* you, to caress *through* you, to think *through* you!

Think of your body as a transmitter of God's holy energy.

You are the light through which God shines.

Open your eyes, look at others, and let God's holy energy be a blessing, shining through you.

As you let God's love work through you, it frees your internal energies so that your dreams become manifest.

Spend your time allowing yourself to grow through God's love.

That's why you're here!

∾ ∾ ∾

Making Space for God

You must create space in order to experience God in your life.

Space in this realm is more accurately defined as time.

God is always aware of you, but you are not always aware of God.

The time you set aside for God allows you to be more conscious of divine presence.

As you become more aware of divine presence, your levels of appreciation, gratitude, and love grow.

Appreciation opens your mind.

Gratitude opens your heart.

Love opens your spirit.

As you open to God's presence, your energies expand so that you become even *more open* to appreciation, gratitude and love.

This shift takes place as you create time to become aware of God.

God is always with you – in every cell, every breath, between every thought.

God adores the essence of your being.

As you open yourself to this adoration, you become a channel for it, so that God's love passes through you into the lives of others.

If you want to be divinely inspired, you must create the space for God to fill.

Begin now.

Practice.

Appreciate, be grateful, and open yourself to God's love.

The Enormity of Your Influence

You are a part of a much larger picture.

Your development, or lack of development, affects *everyone* and *everything*.

You may not comprehend the enormity of your influence at this point in time.

Think of the power a flower has to make you smile!

Remember the joy your favorite song brings you.

Your *natural state* is one of joy, and when you don't allow yourself to connect with this state and cultivate it, you limit the experience of who you are.

The joy you feel as you connect to this part of yourself also connects you to the awareness of the larger cosmic picture.

How can you, like a flower, elicit a smile?

How can you, like a song, produce joy?

Develop these qualities within yourself and they will flow naturally outward, influencing those not only in your immediate proximity, but continuing to flow outward in infinite waves of blessings.

This is how joy flows.

This is how joy grows.

Your part of this cosmic picture is to cultivate the inner ecstasy of who you are.

Overlook weakness and focus on strength.

Develop the beauty of your inner world.

The enormity of your influence will manifest in ways you cannot begin to imagine now!

∽ ∽ ∽

Your Prayers Are Always Answered

Your prayers may not be answered in the way you'd like them to be answered, but they are always honored.

Don't pray with the expectation of being aware of the results.

Your efforts are acknowledged many times more than you may believe.

Your prayers are like music that reverberates endlessly throughout the heavens.

Prayer is a way of allowing your energies to be of service to the Divine.

Prayer connects you to God.

All positive thoughts are a form of prayer.

As you send out positive thoughts they naturally expand and return to you.

Each positive thought you think becomes a prayer that helps transform the negativities in the universe.

Each positive thought is a prayer that caresses the universe with joy.

There is no end to the answering of your prayers!

Live in the Joy of Your Song!

You have music inside of you that makes the angels sing with joy.

Your inner music has a profound resonance that is uniquely yours.

This music is as individual as your thumbprint.

It cannot be duplicated by anyone else.

Learn your inner song.

Learn your inner song and *sing it*.

As you take joy in yourself, you give others permission to take joy in themselves.

Sing, rejoice, and be happy.

Your primary purpose in being on earth is to bring joy into this realm.

Notice the birds.

Allow yourself to experience the joy in their song.

Notice the flowers.

Allow yourself to feel the freshness of each petal.

Notice the trees.

Allow yourself to feel their strength and stability.

Birds, flowers and trees are but a few of the earth's creations that fully live in the joy of their being, in the joy of their song.

Surely humans can do the same!

As you practice being *in joy* you become closer to experiencing the true nature of who you really are.

Practice cultivating joy and your song will emerge.

Sing your song and spread your joy.

221

Don't Take Hurt To Heart

If others hurt you it's because they are reacting to *being* hurt.

They are trying to hurt you in an attempt to externalize their own pain.

If you want to be a conscious, loving human, stop the cycle of negative energy by not accepting their hurt.

Realize that it is not *your* hurt but *theirs*.

Accept *only love* into your life.

Become aware of what loving energy is and what it is not.

As you become familiar with it, it becomes easier to align yourself with its grace.

Loving energy naturally repels negativities.

People who try to hurt you simply don't know any better.

They have been accepting the "gift" of hurt all their lives and they think hurting others is a natural tool to protect them.

They haven't learned that the strongest armor is woven of love.

Teach them about love by aligning yourself with its infinite power.

Teach them about love by allowing this power to deflect any "gifts" of hurt.

As their hurts bounce off you, they will feel the effects of your love, and they'll learn not to inflict pain.

Don't take hurt to heart.

ᔆ ᔆ ᔆ

Turning Emergencies into Opportunities

Sometimes it may seem as if you go from one emergency to the next.

It may seem as if your life is out of control and you have no say in how you spend your time or energy.

Oftentimes it may seem that you are at the mercy of others' whims or needs.

At these times, especially, you must remain centered in God.

These are the times that test your inner connections to divine energy.

They either strengthen you or show you where you need strength.

They humble you in your search for divine truth.

Allow yourself to feel the power of your own choice during these times of stress.

Become aware that you are making the choice to serve others in whatever capacity you are able.

Take your strength back and put it in God's hands.

You are making the decision to allow God to work through you, though you may not understand at this time exactly how God works.

Give yourself to God again.

Feel your strength return as you come back to the empowerment of God's choice.

Turn emergencies into opportunities.

Let God emerge through your 'emerge'-ncies.

Rising Above Betrayal

Everyone experiences betrayal.

Being betrayed helps you to understand how it feels so that you don't betray others.

Betrayal helps you rise above that particular negativity so that you keep your vibrations above that level.

The only value in experiencing betrayal is that you learn you don't want to do it to others.

If you perpetrate "an eye for an eye" you are simply adding strength to negativity.

Your job as an evolving being is to consciously choose kindness, love, and hope.

That means not fostering the return of negativity for negativity, hurt for hurt, blame for blame.

You always have a choice.

You break the cycle of karma when you choose to love in all situations.

You break the cycle of cause-and-effect when you choose kindness over hatred.

You break the cycle of duality when you choose compassion over "getting even."

Your mission is to continually rise above the negative vibrations of envy, resentment, and betrayal.

Sometimes the higher you rise, the greater the challenge.

Don't think of it as getting away from negativity; think of it as *rising up to God*.

The Purpose of Relationships

Relationships are the reason you have chosen to incarnate in this earthly realm.

Relationships allow you to encounter aspects of yourself in the flesh.

They allow you to experience all emotions.

They are the vehicles through which you develop your humanity.

The adage, "Do unto others what you would have them do unto you," serves as a reminder that what you do to others you truly do to a part of yourself.

This adage also allows you to preview the pain or the joy of your actions before you bring them into the physical realm.

Think about how what you say or what you do affects others.

Think about how you would feel if it were said or done to you.

Feel the difference when you say or do something with love verses anger or fear.

Ask what you want to motivate you; love or hurt; joy or pain?

As you learn to come from a positive place within, your relationships will change.

You will become the greater influence in your relationships when you come from a place of love.

That's why you're here.

The Blessing of Recovery

Everyone is recovering from something.

Addictions to food, alcohol, sex, drugs and relationships plague the planet.

These same addictions serve as an opportunity to put you on a spiritual path through recovery.

Overcoming addiction requires a complete shift in the focus of your entire life.

Overcoming addiction requires you to totally and completely change from the inside out.

Addictions require a metamorphosis in order for you to become connected to your soul.

You are on a path of higher learning or you wouldn't be reading this.

You are on a path of *spiritual* evolution, that will serve not only your highest good, but also the highest good of the planet.

Recovery serves as a way of forcing you to become aware of your own limitations and negativities so that you can rise above them.

Recovery serves as a way to find out who you are, why you are here, and how you can fulfill your life's purpose.

Ask yourself what kind of recovery you are in and how it is serving your highest good.

Ask yourself how your recovery is helping you serve the highest good of the planet.

Begin to see recovery for what it truly is: A blessing to all.

Your Real Self Cannot Be Hurt

When someone hurts your feelings, become aware that *what has been hurt is not you.*

You are *not* your feelings.

You feel the hurt because you have identified with your personality.

People try to hurt you in a desperate attempt to feel better because *they have identified* with their personality.

Who you really are cannot be hurt, destroyed, or diminished.

Who you really are can only receive honor, love, and devotion.

You honor your true self by identifying with your holy soul.

As you learn to identify with your holy soul, you learn to honor the holiness in others.

This honoring allows the holiness to grow, both within you and outside of you.

Learn to dismiss the hurt.

Look at being "hurt" as a button that's pushed within you to remind you of your holiness.

Honor your holiness and it will grow.

Honor the hurt and you waste your precious time here.

Always choose love.

Don't let outer appearances deceive you.

As you identify with inner holiness, you automatically correct the false belief that others can hurt you in the first place!

Love Strengthens the Lover

Seek to see the best in others.

Make a choice to focus on their goodness.

As you focus on the good in others, you not only help them to achieve their best, you help to achieve *your* best.

Focusing on the goodness in others naturally raises your own vibration.

What you focus your attention on *grows*.

Focusing your energy on the goodness in others is a form of prayer.

This is the evolutionary force in the universe, because it's based on love.

When you make the decision to see the best in others, you are coming from the motivation of love, the most powerful force in the universe.

That's why the message of Jesus Christ has endured through centuries; He taught us to love our enemies!

Why is it that loving our enemies is *still* a revolutionary idea?

When will we embrace this ancient concept?

We forget that *love strengthens the lover*.

∾ ∾ ∾

Creating Paradise

What is your vision of love?

What is your vision of paradise here on this earth?

What inner vision will help you create this love-filled paradise?

As you cultivate your inner vision, your outer vision unfolds.

Think of all the details you would put in your paradise.

What would your landscape be like?

What colors would surround you?

What would your house look like?

What pets would you have?

Who would you place in your paradise?

What would you do with your time?

What qualities would you have?

How would you treat others?

How would you want to be treated?

The manifestation of your paradise on earth begins *now,* as you energize these ideas with your attention.

Start manifesting with something you know that you can achieve.

Maybe you can bring certain colors into your life.

Maybe you can work on developing personal characteristics, like honesty or compassion.

Create paradise now, based on *your vision* of love.

Love: The Holy Oil of Life

Making the decision *not* to love is what hurts.

Most people are not aware that the decision *not to love* has occurred within them.

When you hurt you may blame it on something or someone outside yourself.

You may think you are in pain because someone has left you, when in actuality; you are in pain because you think you *have to stop loving*.

It is natural to hurt when a loved one leaves you, but your pain can be greatly diminished if you allow yourself to love regardless of external circumstances.

Face the grief.

Embrace it.

Cry until you can't cry any more tears.

Then let the love flow anyway.

Let the love flow from you to the loved one, through the love one, out into the farthest reaches of infinity.

Loving is the most important action you can take, *ever*.

Why would you stop loving when that is what will help you most?

Loving eases pain.

Loving connects you to divine love.

Loving is the healing balm for your grief.

Loving soothes your soul and the souls around you.

Always choose love – the holy oil of life itself.

Pay Attention to Your Angels

Your angels love to be acknowledged, just as you do.

Learn to receive the acknowledgment your angels give to you.

Your angels honor you countless times throughout the day.

Your part of the job is to *pay attention*.

As you honor the blessings they give you, they become more obvious.

Most gifts are subtle: You may receive a nudge to go in a certain direction; an idea may pop into your mind; a gentle breeze may kiss your cheek.

Your angels have total, complete, and unconditional love for you.

They rejoice in your acceptance of their celestial energies.

The more accepting you become of their devotion to you, the stronger the relationship becomes.

Become aware of your angels.

Follow the guidance you receive through your heart.

Pay attention to your angels and their heavenly gifts will become even more obvious.

The Power of Your Words

Language is the vehicle of the mind.

That's why *how you speak to yourself* is so important.

Language opens the door for higher energies to enter your being and raise your consciousness.

As you bring your awareness into each moment, you become conscious of each precious word you are thinking.

Each word is reflected in your outer life.

Each word is a valuable tool used to create your individual reality.

That's why it's important not to take the Lord's, or anyone else's, name in vain.

It's not the divine who suffers when you do so.

Profanities bring down *your* energies and lower *your* awareness.

When you use profanities you remove yourself from the realms of ecstasy and enter the realms of angst.

Does your language nurture or destroy you?

Does your language help or hurt others?

Does your language create heaven or hell on this earth?

Become aware each moment of your language so that you become aware of *how* and *what* you are creating.

The Gift of Anger

Of course you experience anger, just as you experience joy.

There is no point in trying *not* to be angry.

"Trying" itself creates resistance that gives anger power.

Simply recognize anger.

Ask what it *wants* for you.

Anger may want to protect you.

It may want you to protect others.

Anger may want to feed you, keep you safe, or keep you healthy.

It may want you to have love, or peace, or forgiveness.

Anger has a *gift* for you.

Your job is to find out what that gift is.

After you know what the gift is, you can let the anger go.

Every negative has a positive intention.

The quicker you catch yourself experiencing the negative, the sooner you can bring yourself into the positive.

Don't serve anger – allow yourself to receive its gift.

Your Divine Purpose

There is a divine purpose for every soul on this planet.

Once you discover what yours is, your life starts making sense in a whole new way.

Your divine purpose is usually quite simple, but never easy.

Ask yourself, "What am I here to learn?"

Begin to see everything in your life as part of a divine plan that will help you learn your lessons.

Become aware, from this perspective, how beautifully your life has been planned.

Notice how the details of your life have worked together to serve your purpose.

As you see the bigger picture of your life unfold, you begin to understand the saying, "Everything is perfect as it is."

Everything is perfectly designed to help your life's purpose unfold.

Understanding your purpose helps to explain the futility of vengeance, the importance of love, and the treasure of grace.

Why are you here?

Let the beauty and simplicity of your answer permeate your entire being.

As your trust grows your answers flow.

Trust in the holy design of your life's plan.

༄ ༄ ༄

Angel Consciousness

Angel consciousness means being aware, in each moment, of the help you have from the "other side."

As you increase your angel consciousness, you increase your ability to receive help from the other side.

Help comes in many forms.

Sometimes it comes as an inner voice prompting you to do something or take a certain action.

Sometimes it comes as a feather, floating down from the heavens to get your attention.

Sometimes it comes as an incredible sunset to remind you of God's beauty.

Angel consciousness simply means *paying attention* to the subtleties of guidance that you receive.

Your reception is a signal to your angels that you are aware of their presence, and that you are grateful for their guidance.

Being able to receive is a prerequisite to giving.

You can't give freely until you can receive freely.

Developing angel consciousness will help you give and receive.

You are naturally giving and receiving all the time, it's a matter of *what* you are giving and *what* you are receiving.

Receiving love lets you give love.

Let yourself receive the love from your angels so that you can give it to others.

The Mystic's Path

Notice how the sun's light glimmers through the clouds and glistens through the trees.

Notice how the earth sings through the melodies of each soft breeze.

Each bird's song, each flower's sheen, is like a kiss from heaven to you.

This is what *is* personal.

Imagine the heart of each flower expressing devotion to your heart.

Let yourself receive the love each drop of rain is delivering to you.

Accept the caress of the gentle waves of the ocean's bliss.

This is the mystic's path.

This is the mystic's *responsibility*.

My job, your job, is to discover and appreciate the joy in all things.

Become aware of the magnificence in a single breath of air.

Become aware of your own breath bringing life into your body.

Notice the magical ways your energy circulates throughout your entire being.

Become a receiver of love.

Become a dispenser of light.

Get on the mystic's path!

Healing From the Outside In

Regardless of what you feel on the inside, always choose to be loving on the outside.

Learn to say no without bitterness.

Learn to be kind when you need to be firm.

Coming from love doesn't mean you have to say yes.

Coming from love means you have the power to say gently what's in your heart.

Being bitter is a reaction to being hurt.

Being bitter is an attempt to protect your inner wounds from further pain, but it only serves to act like the pathogen it is, infecting your entire being with the poison of negativity.

As you allow yourself to connect with the endless flow of love that exists within, comfort displaces the need to guard hurt with more hurt.

How can hurting more help you to hurt less?

Choose to express love on the outside, and the hurt on the inside will heal.

Your Indelible Print on the Universe

You are either teaching or learning all the time.

Sometimes people are in your life to teach you, and sometimes you are in their lives to teach them.

When a difficult person comes into your life, ask what lessons you have to learn from them.

Chances are *you* are doing the learning.

This is because if you are reading this, you are on a spiritual path, and if you are on a spiritual path, you are actively seeking growth.

Of course, you are *always* teaching.

You are teaching whether you are aware of it or not.

Become aware that every person in your life is a holy person, regardless of appearance.

Let yourself experience the holiness of another.

As you allow yourself to experience this, ask what you are learning from this person.

Ask what you are *teaching* this person.

Are you teaching positive or negative lessons?

Which are you learning?

What do you *want to learn* and what do you *want to teach?*

What indelible imprint are you making on the universe?

Count Your Blessings

The admonition, "Count your blessings," is not said so that you will literally count you blessings.

The implication is that you cannot possibly count your blessings.

You have too many blessings to count!

How could you possibly number the joys that are available to you each day?

The very air you breathe is filled with joy.

Breathe in the sparkles of light and let your entire being appreciate the life force coming into you.

Remember that life is designed to produce the very best, exquisite rose.

Surely the love available to a flower is available to you!

What blessings does a flower have?

Don't you know that the night sky dreams for you?

You must ask yourself what you *want* to dream and the heavens will help you.

Everything in this realm is designed to help you grow.

What is it you need to learn?

Maybe it's simply that you cannot possibly count all your blessings!

Turning Liabilities Into Assets

Sometimes your worst liabilities turn out to be your best assets.

Every liability has its flip side.

What good can possibly come out of having an addiction or being the victim of abuse?

Maybe it's learning to forgive.

Maybe certain liabilities help you become humble.

Maybe they force you into seeking higher levels of consciousness to avoid their pain.

The most important question to answer is, "How does this serve my highest good and the highest good of those around me?"

You do not live in a vacuum.

Everything that affects you affects those around you.

Everything that affects those around you affects you.

Part of your spiritual evolution may be to learn from the liability so that you can help others.

Perhaps it's turning being a victim into being victorious.

Perhaps it's overcoming an addiction so that you get your free will back.

You may learn that you have been on the wise one's path all along; it just took your liabilities to get you there!

Begin to see your liabilities as teachers, and it won't take so long to learn the lessons they have for you.

Once you have learned the lessons, you will understand their role as assets!

The Gifts of Play

What gifts do you have waiting in your heart to emerge?
What delights are inside you waiting to unfold?
What gifts will you help others discover?
You are a vessel of the gifts of joy, delight, and love.
Your job is to *develop* these gifts.
As you do so, you naturally help others develop their own gifts.

Your creative nature is a facet of joy.
What draws your interest?
How do you enjoy spending your time?
What would you do with your time if you didn't "have to" do anything?
How do you play?
Begin to think of playing as a skill that needs to be developed.
Playing allows you to develop joy in productive, meaningful ways.
Playing allows you to develop your gifts and share them with others.
Let yourself play so that your heart's gifts can emerge.

The Blessings Of Angels

Don't ever think you are without help or guidance.

There is never a time when your angels aren't attentive.

There is never a time when angels aren't sending you the energy of their love.

If you knew how much you are loved, you would never be afraid.

Let yourself begin to accept the idea, right at this moment, that you are loved totally and completely.

Let yourself accept the idea now, that your angels know all your secrets, and they love you, not in spite of them, but *because* of them.

Accept your angel's embrace.

Breathe in their heavenly fragrance.

Hear their gentle guidance.

There is no power on earth greater than the love your angels have for you.

You don't have to "do" anything to "get" their love, simply allow yourself to *receive* it.

Let your eyes be blessed with their sight, your ears be blessed with their song, your breath be blessed with their kiss.

There is no fear you cannot conquer with your angels.

There is nothing they cannot help you overcome.

Trust, listen, see, feel, and appreciate their presence.

Your angels are with you always.

Transforming Inadequacies

It is human to feel inadequate.

You may feel that you're not smart enough, good enough, or rich enough.

It's important to acknowledge these feelings when they arise and not let them degenerate into feelings of self-pity.

Self-pity zaps your strength.

The energy that self-pity spawns is like a vortex leading to an endless abyss of darkness.

Self-pity drains any useful energy that you could have used to rise upward.

Catch yourself at the first sign of thinking you're inadequate and ask yourself why you are thinking this way.

Are you comparing yourself to someone else?

You have within you everything you need to become your ideal self.

Comparing yourself to another is setting you up for disaster.

You can admire certain qualities in others and seek to model those qualities, but yearning *to be* another negates the individuality, the unique precious gifts that God gave you.

When you catch yourself feeling inadequate, go deep inside and nurture your unique, positive aspects.

Begin loving yourself all over again.

Talk to yourself as if you were your own best friend.

Remember that you are a unique, one-of-a-kind manifestation of God's love.

It is your *human* nature to feel inadequate but it is your *divine* nature that transforms it.

∾ ∾ ∾

Dissolving Fear

Fear is a knife that stabs the heart.

You can be so terrified that you can't even acknowledge it, and your fear may manifest as panic attacks.

You can become so habituated to fear that you shove it down, deep within yourself until it turns into depression.

On the other hand, some have become so comfortable with fear that it becomes their primary motivation.

See fear as a dark energy spreading throughout your being.

Now envision a loving, golden light coming down through the top of your head and filling your heart, spreading outwards like a starburst, dissolving the darkness of fear.

Allow the golden light to fill every atom of your being.

Think of this light as God's love for you, growing stronger and stronger as you invite it in.

You are filled with the light of divine love.

In this light, there is no room for darkness, for fear.

Fear has been totally replaced with the light of love.

Fear and love cannot exist in the same space, just as darkness cannot exist in the light.

Love yourself as God loves you and see the light become even brighter.

This is the light that dissolves the darkness of fear.

Fill your heart with love so the light within deflects the knife of fear.

~ ~ ~

The Simple Magic of Trust

When you begin to trust your connection to God, your life will begin to change like magic.

Go deep inside and tap into that inner knowing, that inner feeling of connection to the universe.

Experience how good it feels to connect to the earth.

Breathe in the very sky itself!

Don't put your trust in a person.

Put your trust in God alone.

When your trust is anchored in God, you can begin to trust yourself.

When you become aware that your existence in this universe is *necessary,* your doubts will vanish like dust in the wind.

Regardless of what *appears* to be, know that you are here to manifest your highest potential, and that the universe is set up to *help you* do just that.

You don't have to believe what you thought as a child.

If those beliefs serve your highest good, wonderful!

But if they don't, you have the choice to discard them and create new beliefs.

If you weren't taught to trust in God, make the decision to trust now.

Make the decision to turn to God in moments of doubt.

Understand that you trusted the universe when you came here, and you can trust the universe now.

Trust creates a magical energy that draws just the right people, places and things to you.

Trust, and watch the magic of your life unfold.

∽ ∽ ∽

If You Don't Let Go, You Won't Grow

Become aware of your need to be right.

Think of a situation in which it was important for you to prove how right you were.

Now go deep inside and remember how that energy felt.

Notice how the need to be right feels.

It's strong, stubborn, and rigid.

Hanging onto this need keeps you stuck.

It keeps you in an infantile mode of stagnation, as if you were in a permanent posture of flailing your arms, screaming and gritting your teeth!

Now let that feeling go.

Surrender it to God's energy for transformation.

Feel the rigidity being replaced with the comfort of flexibility.

Allow the suppleness of trust to return to your being.

Feel the spark of growth returning as you allow yourself to fall into the arms of God's love.

Growth is by nature a process.

Your need to prove yourself right stunts your growth.

In the overall scheme of things, what does it matter?

Notice the sense of freedom you feel as you let go of this need.

And now be thankful that God is transforming this energy for you.

The more you surrender, the more God can transform.

If you don't let go, you won't grow.

Who Feels What You Think?

Who *feels* what you *think* about another?
Who *feels* what you *speak* about another?
You do!
That's why it is so important to think and speak in a positive manner regardless of whom you are thinking or speaking about, including *yourself!*

The levels of manifestation are first; thinking, second; feeling, and third; action.

Your thinking determines your feelings, and your feelings determine your actions.

If you want to feel good, think positive thoughts.

If you speak ill of another, you are feeling the energy of those ill thoughts.

If you speak lovingly of another, you are feeling the vibrations of those loving thoughts.

Decide how you want to feel, and then begin thinking thoughts that create those feelings!

It takes practice to be the master of your feelings, but you can begin to think about this practice as exciting and fun!

In time, you will have created a pattern of experiencing happiness and joy!

The more you practice, the easier it gets, and the sooner you will recognize negative thoughts when they arise.

You are going to be using your mind anyway, so you might as well use it to create happy, joyful feelings!

How do you want to feel?

Be aware, practice, and create the miracle of happiness in your life!

∽ ∽ ∽

Your Holy Self

Go deep inside yourself until you connect with God's love for you.

The need to connect with this eternal, unending, all-powerful energy is in everyone and can only be fulfilled by going within.

You may be afraid to go within because you may be afraid of what you'll find there, because you identify with what's *wrong* with you rather than what's *right* with you.

You haven't discovered who you really are.

You may think you are your anger, your resentments, or your stubbornness.

When you go deep inside and become aware of who you are on a soul level, you become absolutely overwhelmed with love.

As you go beyond the fear, you get to experience the love.

Who you really are is holy beyond your imaginings.

You cannot even dream of how fabulous your inner beauty is.

The negativity and the fear form a veil of illusion you must walk through in order to reveal your true self.

Don't resist this illusion.

Don't fight it.

Become aware of what it is and go beyond it.

Your holy inner-self, which is an expression of divine love, is shining through the darkness of this illusion.

Go within and connect with your holy self, God's love made flesh.

෴ ෴ ෴

Enter God's Bliss

Find something that you love to do.
Find something that makes your heart sing.
Participate in this activity regularly.
Do it for the pure joy it gives you.
Don't do it to become *good* at it.
Just do it for the *pleasure* it brings you.

This may be something simple, like watching butterflies, reading, seeing a movie, listening to music, participating in a sport, fishing, cooking - anything that you enjoy.

Learn to value joy for what it is: A vital ingredient in your life.

The universe is filled with delights!

Allow yourself to experience them, as they are solace for the soul.

They raise your energy.

They are food for the heart.

When you connect with what gives you joy, you are doing what you're supposed to be doing.

You are not "supposed" to experience pain, drudgery, or dissatisfaction.

Those are by-products of *not* following your dreams.

As you delight in yourself, you delight in God.

Give up your suffering and enter into God's bliss.

If you think God wants you to be sad in order to grow, you will spend your whole life courting misery.

Delight in the small things and let them fill your life with joy, which is God's plan for you anyway!

Your Divine Duty

You may think it is your duty to be sad.

If you have lost a loved one, gone through a break-up, suffered a grave or chronic illness, you may think that the joy in your life is over and that you can never feel happy again.

Grief is a condition of being human.

Your job is to grow *through* the grief.

Embrace it, examine it, feel it, and then *let it go*.

Walk through it so that you emerge on the other side.

Find that pinpoint of light in the darkness of grief.

Allow that light to get brighter.

Allow that light to get brighter until it is the sun of your universe, illuminating the darkness as only the sun can.

This doesn't mean that you will never experience sadness again, but as the night turns to day, sadness can melt away, getting smaller and smaller and smaller.

Your duty is to let the sadness go.

Grief may be a part of life, but it is *only a part*.

Your job is not to get stuck there.

Focus on the tiny dot of light.

Keep an element of joy within you.

Death, destruction and disease do not equal failure.

They represent passages, changes, and opportunities you must face on your journey.

When the darkness comes, simply know that it's there, and step into the light.

Always go toward the light.

Your duty is not to be sad.

Your divine duty is to cultivate joy through the sadness.

Who Are You?

Who are you?
Are you your body?
Are you your mind?
Are you your feelings?
Are you the thoughts that run through your head like little monkeys swinging from treetops in the jungle?
Are you the anger that you feel toward another when your power is usurped?
Are you the heart that gets broken, the thinking that can't figure it out, the head that won't stop hurting?
Do you know what you are?
Do you know what you *are not?*
When you connect with who you *really are*, your life will unfold in an entirely new way.
The dawn of understanding will shine a different light on your life.
As you see yourself in this way, you can make different choices based on wisdom and understanding.
When you know who you are, you can ask *why* you are here.
What did you come here to learn?
What is your life's purpose?
Who would you *like* to be?
What kind of energy would you like to generate?
What is your highest ideal of yourself?
How does it feel to express your highest potential?
Who are you?

The Hidden Joys Along Your Path

Imagine walking along a path.

As you walk along it, your job is to discover joy, and uncover hidden delights.

This is a *new* journey for you.

You've never been on this path before.

Some of the areas may seem familiar, but it's really unexplored.

You are like an explorer as you venture down this road, discovering treasures everywhere!

It may seem at times that you've taken a wrong turn, that there are obstacles in the path that prevent you from continuing.

These obstacles, however, were really put there to test your creative skills.

Where is the joy this obstacle is hiding?

As you detour around this obstacle, what new delights do you discover that you wouldn't have if the obstacle hadn't been there?

How is this obstacle allowing you to see your life from a fresh, new perspective?

How is this obstacle helping you discover truths about yourself?

Now, from this vantage point, notice how the obstacle seems like a *gift* that was placed in your path, *just for you.*

This obstacle is a personal gift from the universe that allows you to see things about yourself, to grow in unique ways, to discover new delights that otherwise you would have overlooked.

Joy is the fuel that propels you to discover even more joy.

What joys will you discover on today's path?

Only Love is Real

Nothing that is truly real can be destroyed.

Physical things are only outer manifestations of energy, and energy can be *transformed*, but not destroyed.

The body can be reduced to ash, but the soul in the body is never destroyed; it's released.

The soul in the body exists in realms that *cannot* cease to exist.

Fear develops when you attach your reality to appearances, to what *appears* to be real.

What's real is the love that souls share.

What hurts is when you try to suppress that love.

What's real exists forever, that's why you can't destroy love.

Allow the energy of love to flow through you.

Don't try to stop it, no matter how you perceive *appearances*.

Don't be concerned with love being returned.

Love will return to you as long as *you don't stop* loving.

It has to, because love follows the same course as all energy.

Love *returns to the sender.*

Let your love flow outward and it will return to you.

Regardless of appearances, what cannot be destroyed, your soul, allows the energy of love to flow outward.

This energy flow is never destroyed, but it returns to you as long as you keep the flow going.

That's why cultivating love is the most important thing you can do!

Signs From God

Most people want a sign from God.

Most people want to know that they are headed in the right direction, that they have His approval, that they have His love.

Sometimes you may feel so low, you think you need a big sign, like, "I love you!" written across the sky in clouds.

If you pay attention, however, you are sure to become aware of countless little signs around you.

When you ask a question of the Divine, *trust* that it will be answered, but give up any expectations as to exactly *how* it should be answered.

Don't try to *find* the answer; trust that the answer will *come* to you.

Don't *demand* an answer or a sign; just be willing to *receive* it, on whatever level it's presented to you.

Thank the Divine for this information *before* you have actually received it.

Gratitude raises your vibrations so that you're more likely to be aware of whatever is given to you.

Be willing to go through a period in which you *don't know*.

Accept this unknowing and be grateful for it, knowing that this is part of the process.

Pay attention.

Become aware of the signs God is giving you.

∽ ∽ ∽

It's *Only* a Thought

You are *not* your thinking.

You are *not responsible* for what thoughts pop into your mind.

You are, however, responsible for what *you do* with those thoughts once they are in your mind.

If a bizarre or unpleasant thought occurs to you, what do you do with it?

If you try to fight it, it gets stronger.

You actually give it more energy when you try to *stop* the thought from entering your mind.

Ignoring it doesn't work either, because ignoring the thought is like trying to pretend it's not there in the first place.

One effective way to deal with unwanted thoughts is to acknowledge them, and then become aware that they are *not* coming *from you.*

You did *not* create the unwanted thought, or it wouldn't be unwanted.

As it comes into your consciousness, see it for what it is, and notice as it drifts away.

It's only a thought.

As you let go of unwanted thoughts, *cultivate* the *wanted* thoughts.

Cultivate thoughts that enrich your life, that make you feel good, that help you achieve your goals.

As you practice, your negative, unwanted thinking will diminish and you will find yourself getting closer to your goals as your positive thoughts increase.

You are not your thinking, but you *can choose* what thoughts you want to develop.

When Does Your Soul Sing?

It's not what is *outside* of you that is important; it's what's *inside*.

The beauty, the riches and the treasures in this world are also in your heart.

"The kingdom of heaven is within," is more than a metaphor.

As you go within and develop your own resources, outer manifestations will take on a whole new meaning.

What kind of beauty do you value?

What is your strongest wish?

When do you feel your best, on *all levels* of your being?

What do you enjoy doing that has nothing to do with anyone else?

What are you thinking when you are the happiest you can be?

When does your soul sing?

When do you feel closest to God?

As you discover these things, notice how they are related to what is *inside* of you.

Become aware of what you need to develop in your life in order to experience these higher states of being.

Begin *now*.

Start with the thought that brings you the greatest joy.

Let it fill your heart and expand outward and outward, beyond the beyond.

Start where you are and continue, each instant, to nurture your inner treasures.

Your inner treasures are what you are here to develop.

When does your soul sing?

Your Gifts are Vital

You are the *only person* on this planet who can express your gifts.

You may have the gift of compassion; so important to give when others are hurting.

You may have the gift of calmness; so necessary when chaos is around you.

You may have the ability to smile in the midst of an intense situation, alleviating fear at just the right moment.

Perhaps your sense of humor helps defray overwhelming tension.

Maybe you have the ability to pray on another's behalf.

Maybe you have the gift of appreciating beauty, no matter where you find yourself.

Perhaps you can sense when another needs help.

Maybe you can contribute to the needy, grow flowers for the ill, or cook for the hungry.

Thank God for whatever gifts you have and be open for opportunities to use them.

You never know when your gifts can make a difference in the lives of others.

Only you can express *your gifts.*

The more you are thankful and the more you give, the greater your positive influence is on this world.

As you give your gifts away, they multiply.

What are your vital gifts?

Discover Yourself

Become aware of where your energies are.

Are they flitting from place to place, in between focusing on these words?

What is pulling at your energy?

What draws away your attention?

Is your attention the same as your thoughts?

How can you achieve mastery over yourself if you don't have control over your attention?

What will help you learn to focus?

Do you have the ability to choose where your attention goes?

Begin to see your thinking as a great inner resource that only you can develop.

One way you can develop this resource is by learning to focus it.

This is a simple, yet crucial, step.

The practice of meditation will help you develop the inner wealth of your mind.

Meditation will allow you to focus your attention so that you can *choose* how to think, *how* to use your mind.

Meditation allows you to become aware of your thinking so that you can choose where to invest your energies.

Meditation allows you to begin the inner journey of discovering who you really are.

Practice.

Become aware of your thoughts.

Discover yourself.

Don't Give Up, Let Go!

There is a difference between *letting go* and *giving up*.

Letting go implies a trust in God that everything will be okay.

Giving up implies a resignation of the soul.

Letting go releases the need to control an outcome.

Letting go of future outcomes allows you to experience the *joys of now*.

Each precious moment that you live in trust, you live in love.

When you trust God enough to let Him take over your life, you open the door to His eternal love.

Give Him your anger, your mistrust, and your jealousy.

Give Him your worries, concerns, and frustrations.

Do you think you can do a better job solving your problems than He can?

Surrender to divine guidance and let God control your life.

Don't give up, let go!

∾ ∾ ∾

Turning Hatred Into Adoration

God never stops showering you with grace.

There has never been a *single moment* in your life that He has withheld his infinite love for you.

You may not always have been *aware* of it.

You may have, at times, turned away from it.

But God's eternal grace has *always* been there for you.

Your soul's development takes an enormous leap forward when you recognize and accept this divine grace.

Awareness of His all-encompassing love helps you develop love *for yourself*.

After all, if the most powerful force in the universe loves you, shouldn't you love yourself, too?

As you accept God's love, you begin to flourish in a whole new way.

You recognize that your cup overflows.

As you recognize divine grace working in your life, you open the door for even *more* expressions of this exquisite energy.

All you have to do is trust that grace is always with you.

This grace helps you let go of the petty anger, resentments, and jealousies that prevented you from loving yourself.

As you let go of hating yourself, you release the blocks to your awareness of your true nature.

You can accept this infinite flow of creativity and love.

Your hatred can turn into adoration, another aspect of God's grace.

As you learn to love yourself, you learn to love God and accept His grace, which always has been and always will be in your life.

ꭥ ꭥ ꭥ

When Life Doesn't Work

Sometimes it may seem as if nothing is working in your life.

Sometimes it may seem as if life is just too hard to keep going.

You may wonder where God is, where your angels are.

You may feel alone and powerless.

That's when it's even more important to, "Trust in the Lord with all thy heart; and lean not unto thy own understanding." (Proverbs 3:5)

You can't see the big picture from your vantage point.

Your understanding in this realm is limited, and this is what causes grief.

Despair is the result of a limited perspective.

Your perspective is limited because you exist in the relative realm, where everything is limited!

That's why meditation is so important; it raises your consciousness into a higher plane where perceptual shifts (miracles) are possible.

That's what God-consciousness is all about.

If you want to maintain human-consciousness, *don't meditate!*

Meditation can be dangerous for humans because it rocks the boat of relative reality.

Meditate, if you dare, and release yourself from human-consciousness.

Meditate, enter the realms where miracles are created, and watch your life start working again.

Don't Fall for Jealousy

Look beyond the veil of separation and see all others as *aspects of you.*

This is especially helpful when experiencing jealousy.

Instead of being resentful when someone has what you want, think, "I'm so glad that aspect of me is enjoying such-and-such."

It can be anything this person has that you want: A beautiful partner, a fabulous attitude, a house on the beach, a luxury car, a happy family - anything!

The next time you catch your mind falling into jealousy, turn it around and think how happy you are that part of you is enjoying this wonderful thing that *used to* make you jealous.

It may seem like a trick, and that's exactly what it is.

It's a trick to help your mind from falling to a lower level of consciousness.

When you truly realize we are all one, you'll realize it's not a trick to accept others as reflections of you, because, in fact, they are.

That's when you can give up the tricks of the mind, of which jealousy is only one.

Allow yourself to perceive beyond the limitations of the mind, where jealousy doesn't exist!

Change Your Thinking, Change Your Feeling

How do you change the way you feel?

Begin with changing the way you think.

When you feel sad, depressed, angry, or resentful, pay attention to the *thoughts* running through your mind.

Identify *one thought*.

Chances are it's negative.

Replace that negative thought with two positive thoughts.

It may seem at first as if you are lying to yourself, so make the positive thoughts true and believable.

They may be thoughts such as, "I have the ability to change my thinking," or, "I am on a path of spiritual growth."

Keep the thoughts short and in the present tense.

Notice how it *changes* the way you *feel*.

Only you can change your thinking.

Only you can change your feelings.

What are you thinking now?

∽ ∽ ∽

Let Love Power Your Prayers

Don't ever underestimate the power of prayer, one of the most important actions you can take.

By sending loving thoughts to others you are helping them manifest their ideal.

When you pray for others, see them strong and full of light. Visualize them at their best.

Regardless of what seems to be real in this dimension, know that they are complete, whole, and healed in the realms beyond the walls of illusion.

You can help others manifest their perfection by knowing that they *are* perfect, in total alignment with love.

Every time you think of others as perfect expressions of God, you are helping them create their highest good.

Whether you think your prayers are "working" or not, your positive intentions are helping; the energy of love is never wasted.

You may never know in this realm exactly how your prayers have been utilized, but their power is important beyond your knowledge.

Let love be the energy that powers your prayers, and don't underestimate *your power* to help!

❧ ❧ ❧

Change, One Thought at a Time

Since a belief is something that can change, is a belief true?
Can truth change?
Can your beliefs change?
Are your beliefs helping you be who you want to be?
Or are your beliefs limiting you?
What do you believe would help you achieve your goals?
What is one thing you can do now that will help you manifest your dreams?

You can begin to change your life by identifying what *thoughts* are limiting you.

Every time you catch yourself thinking a limiting thought, *change it.*

Change that thought into one that is accurate, yet positive.

You might change the thought, "This is too hard," into, "I am getting better at this!"

Keep up this practice.

Notice that change begins *one thought at a time.*

Notice that *you can change* one thought at a time.

෨ ෨ ෨

Replace Fear With Faith

Notice how you feel as you enter into different states of mind.

Notice that when you become agitated, your thinking is scattered and you seem to have no control.

Your heart beats faster, your breathing increases, your muscles tense.

Your energies contract and pull inward as you go into the "fight or flight" response.

Now notice how you feel when you enter a meditative state of mind.

Notice the calmness that permeates your entire being.

Feel the waves of soothing energy as your consciousness expands.

Faith replaces fear as you tap into this universal field.

The unlimited field of consciousness becomes your playground.

There are no limits!

Notice how your body feels.

Notice the stillness within.

Notice that it is your thinking - rather, your *lack of thinking* – that allows this state of consciousness to occur.

Become aware of how wonderful it feels to be in touch with your energies in this manner.

Notice how good it feels to *be you*.

Practice noticing.

Practice stillness.

The more you practice, the easier it is to be the *authentic you*, experiencing this wonderful state.

Practice, and faith will replace fear.

Internal Time and External Time

There are two kinds of time: Internal time and external time.

External time is what you do with your body; internal time is what you do with your mind.

Many occupy internal time with external devices, such as T.V., radio, music, or reading.

All those things can be useful, but do you save any internal time to spend with yourself?

It's not a matter of being selfish; it's a matter of being smart.

How can you begin to know yourself if you don't spend time with yourself?

How can you develop spiritually if you fill your internal time with external distractions?

Spending time alone, internally, is one of the most valuable things you can do.

You may know yourself on the outside, but do you know yourself on the inside?

Basically, all *you have is time* and the freedom to choose *what to do* with that time.

When those two abilities are *consciously combined*, *unlimited powers* become available.

Learning how to use limited external time prepares you for using unlimited internal time.

So, how do you use your time?

❦ ❦ ❦

Bring Heaven to Earth

Everyone has different lessons to learn and different skills to share with others.

It is important that you *allow* yourself to be unique.

How else can you develop your soul?

Honoring yourself for who you are and who you are becoming is crucial to your growth.

If there is such a thing as a mistake, it is the mistake of not appreciating who you *really are*.

You came here to express individual aspects of divine energy.

As you develop the ability to express these, you overcome your limitations.

If you accept the idea that you *chose* these limitations to help develop your divine aspects, your life will flow more easily and comfortably.

Your life is not designed to make you suffer, but to help you grow *beyond* suffering.

As you learn to express your individual gifts in spite of your limitations, your suffering diminishes.

Focus on the gifts and they will grow.

Focus on the limitations, and you will suffer.

Focus on your gifts and the gifts of others, and you bring heaven to earth.

∾ ∾ ∾

Cultivate Your Silence

Listen to the sounds of the universe.

The sounds of the universe are heard when you go deep within, beyond your own, inner silence.

External sounds interfere with inner silence, which is why it is so important to experience quiet.

Notice how being quiet and being still are synonymous.

External sound is a vibration, a physical movement.

At first, the quiet may be frightening, because you think you are alone.

External sound has the quality of helping you *feel* that you are not alone.

Of course, you are never alone, but you may not know that yet.

As you go through your internal silence, you may experience glorious heavenly realms.

These realms coexist alongside ordinary realms, but are difficult to experience without the aid of silence.

Let silence be your ally.

Cultivate your silence so you can hear the sounds of the universe.

ᖆ ᖆ ᖆ

Turn Off Your Inner Judge

How do you *think* about yourself?

What is the first thought that popped into your mind when you read that question?

Become aware of your *first reaction to yourself*, because it determines all of your other actions.

All subsequent reactions to this first thought will attempt to justify it.

Since you don't want to spend your inner time defending who you think you are, it's important to develop an honest, loving way to look at yourself.

This allows you to experience forgiveness, grace, and compassion.

When you see yourself in this way, there is nothing to defend.

You won't need to spend internal time defensively, so you'll have much more energy to be creative and loving.

Imagine your life without that awful inner judge.

This is the state of being you want to cultivate.

This is who you really are, without the harshness, cynicism, and negativity that you thought were you.

Your life begins with you.

Change the way you think about yourself, and watch your life change.

ᗢ ᗢ ᗢ

Hearing the Echoes of God's Voice

Music can be like a friend.

The sound of music can be a companion, a presence in your life that keeps you from loneliness.

Any sound can serve that purpose, which is why some people are so uncomfortable with silence.

Many people have no idea what to do with their thoughts, so they must constantly surround themselves with sound.

Becoming comfortable with silence allows you the opportunity to become comfortable with yourself.

You are not your thinking, but your thinking has a great deal of influence over what you manifest.

That's why becoming aware of it is so crucial to your soul's development.

Your internal thinking can serve as internal sound, which can exist to make you feel as if you are not alone.

You will truly realize you are not alone when you quiet both the internal and external noise, for it is then that you can hear the echoes of God's voice.

God speaks softly, like a petal floating on a breeze.

Let God's voice be your music, and your best friend.

∽ ∽ ∽

Watch All Fear Disappear

Of what are you most afraid?

One of the biggest fears people have is the fear of not being loved.

The terror that this thought creates is beyond all other terrors.

It's as if you would *cease to exist* without love - and you *would*.

There would be no energy upon which your soul could live without love.

There is a secret to overcoming this fear that all the saints and holy ones know.

The secret is this: To overcome the fear of not being loved, *you must love*.

It's that simple.

It's *not* important that others *love you*.

What's important is that *you love others*.

When you love others, who feels the love?

As you allow the divine energy of love to flow through you, it multiplies.

The more you love, the more you can love.

Allow love to flow through you and watch all your fears disappear.

෨ ෨ ෨

Becoming Aware of God's Grace

God's grace is all around you, like the air you breathe.

It does not discriminate; it is there for everyone.

Your job is to recognize its presence and to appreciate its gift.

God's grace is experienced in different ways:

A stranger's smile.

Time spent with loved ones.

Time spent alone.

It may be just the right words coming from *your mouth* at just the right time.

You may be a gift from God in someone else's life, and not know it.

God's graces are everywhere.

The more aware you become, the more you can recognize the gifts.

As you evolve spiritually, you'll realize that it is only through God's grace that you are able to read these words, and it is only through God's grace that I am able to write them.

Breathe in God's grace and grow!

ᕦ ᕦ ᕦ

Turn to God First

You may forget that the *first* thing to do is to trust in God, not the *last* thing.

You may exhaust all possibilities, all avenues of understanding, and then think, "Well, I'll just have to trust God. I'll just have to have faith that everything will work out."

You could save yourself an enormous amount of suffering if you would turn to God *first*.

The point of learning to live in the moment, of grounding yourself, is to always keep God "in mind."

With God "in mind," you are experiencing the highest form of consciousness.

Being conscious that you are in the mind of God allows you to be a channel of heavenly brilliance.

This brilliance is coming through you; you are not its source.

This is "getting out of your own way."

When you let go of your ego self, you become an avenue of celestial wisdom and understanding.

The need to be "right," the need to "know," the need for anything, is part of the ego.

That's the importance of giving up desire.

Desires are ego "needs."

Turn to God *first*.

Live with God "in mind."

Be a channel of heavenly brilliance.

∽ ∽ ∽

Your Field of Joy

Joy is all around you.

It is up to you to expand your personal energy field into the field of joy.

Joy exists in a leaf that changes from summer's green to autumn's golden light; in the growth of a single blade of grass, bursting through the earth.

There is a delight to behold in the clear red of a cardinal's feather.

Deepest happiness emerges in the fragrance of the tiniest, palest flowers.

There is bliss in the dark bark that surrounds the strong, tall trees.

There is an explosion of joy in each drop of rain as it splashes on the ground with abandon.

There is no end to this feast of delights!

Sorrows vanish like shadows in the morning sun as your energies merge with joy.

There is no place you can go without these delights.

Simply open your soul to these healing energies.

Bliss is all around you, all the time, waiting for you to breathe it in, like gulps of ecstasy!

What is your capacity for joy?

The more you allow yourself to experience happiness the greater your capacity for joy becomes.

You exercise your happiness by tuning into the ever-present joy around you.

Become bliss!

Expand your field of joy!

Your First Thought

Allow your first thought upon awakening to be of God.

Thanking God is the beginning of enlightenment.

Thanking God reminds you of *who you are* and *why you are here.*

Gratitude puts you on the infinite circle of co-creation and majesty.

When you allow God to be your first awareness, all thoughts that follow are holy.

God is the foundation and first cause of everything in your life.

As you honor this knowledge, you begin to see the holiness and goodness in all things.

This is important not for God, but *for you.*

Who feels the honor you give the divine?

You do!

As you generate thanks to God, gratitude flows through your being in an infinite beam of light-energy.

You exist at the point where contrast, where yin/yang meets, where eternity turns and touches itself.

Gratitude and thoughts of God help you become a generator of light-energy, which returns to itself, *you!*

You become the receiver and the giver at the *same time!*

This is the crux of divine paradox.

The place where you become aware of God is *within you!*

Thank God!

Be a generator of light.

Let your first thought be of God and all goodness will follow.

Despair

Sometimes sadness steals moments before you realize what happened.

Sorrow can overwhelm life like the floods of a storm; so intense and powerful that you feel there is no escape.

At such times, you may experience the deluge of despair.

You may feel that you *have always been sad*, and that you *will always be sad*.

Happiness, joy, and delight are words, but they are not real in these times because they are not felt.

The lightness of being is like a cosmic joke played upon the darkness of the mind.

You become heavy with relentless fatigue and feel as if you could sink into the earth's core.

These are the times when you have *forgotten who you really are*.

You have identified with your body, mind, or feelings.

You are *not* these things.

You have come here to *experience* these things.

When you *forget* you are a child of God, you can't help but fall into darkness and despair.

Your soul's grace is *awareness*.

The depths of despair only claim you when you lose awareness of your true identity: A spiritual being created to live in joy!

When the floods of sadness threaten to drown you, remember *who you really are*.

Your job is to rise above thinking and allow your awareness to expand into the divine realms of bliss - where grief, sadness and despair *cannot* exist.

Be Thankful

When you feel really low, remember to be thankful.

As you begin to notice things to appreciate, you turn from sadness to bliss.

Start with simple things.

Even if you don't really feel it, begin expressing thanks for all you have taken for granted.

Be thankful for awakening in the morning.

Be thankful for the first food that touches your lips.

Be thankful for the bed or cot or mat or floor or earth upon which you sleep.

Give thanks for the meat, or plants, that provide your nourishment.

Give thanks that you can read or hear or feel the messages written here.

Be thankful for the air that fills your lungs, the blood that fills your veins, the love that fills your heart.

Allow this grace to fill you, expand your consciousness, and elevate you above the lows of temporal perception.

As you expand into grace, you naturally rise and burst through the confines of earthly contrast into heavenly bliss.

For what do you have to be thankful?

෴ ෴ ෴

The Rattle of the Mind

The rattle of the mind is a great deception.

The analysis and justifications zap your energies in an endless cycle of attack and retreat.

This method of dealing with the mind doesn't work because the nature of the process is duality.

The only way the mind can experience true peace is to *rise above* contrast.

Contrast and duality create the rattle of the mind.

The material mind is fickle and flits from positive to negative.

The higher consciousness of divine mind allows a perspective that is beyond human duality.

The secret to experiencing peace is to experience both realities at the same time.

As a human, you will never entirely escape contrast.

Indeed, it's one of the reasons you are here.

As spiritual beings, you are naturally drawn to God-consciousness.

As human-spirits, you can only experience God-consciousness when the rattle of the mind is still.

As you experience this stillness, the truth of your divine nature is revealed and you experience oneness.

The perception of duality is lifted and the bliss of eternal oneness is realized.

Don't fight the rattle of the mind, rise above it.

Always Choose Love

The choices that you make based in love come back to bless you a thousand times.

They lead you to a level of consciousness that transcends the physical.

This mystical state unfolds naturally as you continue to choose the higher frequencies of love.

It is a portal through which unlimited knowledge and wisdom flow.

Love is the first and the last choice you must make in order to live in this spiritual flow.

Before you speak, before you act, ask yourself, "Am I coming from love?"

Notice as you travel into the frequencies of love, all the relationships, all the circumstances in your life take on a brighter light.

Your life becomes more manageable.

Relationships become more agreeable.

Circumstances become easier to handle.

As you continue to choose love in each moment, each succeeding moment becomes filled with ease.

Choosing love allows you the luxury of *continuing* to choose love.

When you consider the alternatives, why would you choose anything but love?

∾ ∾ ∾

Self-Mastery

Self-mastery begins with the first thought.

The first thought in your mind that you give energy to is the thought that grows and develops.

This thought has the potential to help you achieve who you want to become, or to reduce you to your deepest fears.

You give the thought energy by "paying" attention to it.

You may not have control over what thoughts pop into your mind, but you do have control over what you do with those thoughts.

If an unwanted thought pops into your mind, you simply acknowledge it and dismiss it.

Don't react emotionally because the emotion gives it power.

Simply notice the unwanted thought, and if it helps you to dismiss it, visualize putting it in a trash can, like the trash can in your kitchen or on your computer screen.

Immediately put your attention on a wanted thought, a positive thought, or a thought that represents you fulfilling a dream or desire.

Let that positive thought grow into another positive thought.

Keep the chain of positive thoughts growing.

This is how you create your reality.

This is how you manifest self-mastery: One thought at a time.

᠗ ᠗ ᠗

Fear and Anger

When you are overcome with anger, ask yourself, "What am I afraid of?"

Many times anger is a cover-up for fear.

Anger may motivate action, while fear may paralyze.

It's much easier to deal with anger than fear.

When you come to terms with your fears the anger vanishes like fog in brilliant sunshine.

Wisdom brings the courage to admit your fears and work through them.

How is your greatest fear affecting your daily life?

What would happen if it actually manifested?

How would your life change?

How much of your energy are you giving this fear on a moment-to-moment basis?

How would your life change if you *weren't afraid*?

What would happen to you?

What would you do with all the energy you'd have that you're now devoting to fear?

Why not start now?!

Just for *this moment*, decide to let go of fear.

Feel the freedom of that decision, *just for this moment*.

Now move into the *next moment*.

If the fear comes back, make the decision to let it go.

Feel the freedom, the relief, and the expansion of energy as you choose to release fear.

Each moment without fear is a moment fully lived.

The Gifts of This Temporal Realm

One of the reasons you are on earth is to learn about the temporal nature of this realm.

Material things are a reflection of your spiritual nature, but they are not its highest form.

The energies that you are aware of in this realm are limited, but it's crucial that you understand them.

Without an understanding of these energies, you can't function at optimum levels.

That's why it's important to appreciate each moment, each breath, and each step you take.

On earth, you experience the limitations of physical laws because of the wisdom you can learn through the limitations.

Limitations serve as guidelines to help keep you focused and grounded.

Look at all the limitations in this realm as self-imposed gifts.

What can you learn from these "gifts" that you can't learn any other way?

What is the message these gifts are teaching you?

As you understand these messages, you grow.

It's like a plant using fertilizer to mature to its greatest potential.

How is your "fertilizer" helping you grow?

∾ ∾ ∾

As you Remember, You Become

Take a moment and go deep inside.

Take a deep breath, get quiet, and contact that part of you that knows the universe is in perfect order.

Now, from this perspective of knowing, look back on your life.

Become aware that everything *had to happen* the way it happened in order for your life to be as it is *right now*.

All the "mistakes" you thought you made weren't mistakes at all - they were steps that led you to where you are today.

Each decision you made brought you to your present state.

Even though you might choose not to make the same choices if you had to do it over again, you wouldn't have that knowledge *unless* you had made those choices *then*.

It's important to enjoy *whatever you can enjoy*, now, in this moment.

The more you *appreciate* the past and let go of its hurts, the more you are able to appreciate the present.

The more you appreciate the present, the more joy you experience in each moment.

Each joyful moment experienced now creates a past that can be remembered with joy.

Let the negativities of the past go; they're gone anyway.

Be joyful *now*.

∽ ∽ ∽

Soul Music

Listen to your inner music.

The melodies you hear with your inner ears are infinitely more wondrous than anything you can hear on the outside.

Your inner music is so fabulous because it is uniquely in harmony with your intrinsic vibrations.

Your soul has its own individual vibrations that exist *only through you.*

Once you get in tune with yourself, everything else takes on a different tone.

Getting in tune with yourself requires stilling the chatter of the mind so the internal music can be heard.

Don't "try" to listen.

Just listen.

This inner hearing is a natural consequence of being connected, on all levels, to the earth, to others, and to your divine nature.

Even if you are totally deaf in the physical realms, you can tune into your inner music.

You are like an individual tuning fork that beautifully expresses unique, fantastic tones.

These tones can't be duplicated in the earthly realms, but they can be recognized and appreciated.

Quiet the outside so you can listen to the inside.

Honor your song and it will develop into a symphony - a symphony that can only be expressed *through you.*

ᕦ ᕦ ᕦ

Inner Treasures

If you don't have a rich inner life, it doesn't matter how rich your outer life is.

External riches can never replace internal poverty.

As you develop inner resources, outer resources will naturally develop.

What is your most valuable inner asset?

What do you prize most about yourself?

How do you develop this inner treasure?

What do you do to help your inner treasures grow?

How are the dividends of these inner assets manifesting in your life?

One interesting quality about inner valuables is that, like outer valuables, they grow as you invest them properly.

In order for your inner riches to grow, you must "pay" attention to them.

As you "spend" time developing inner resources, your cup can't help but overflow.

External riches take on a whole new perspective as you learn their true purpose.

How much do you have invested in your inner treasures?

What are *you worth* to you?

Begin by valuing *who you are now*, at this moment.

Pay attention and watch your inner treasures grow.

How to Make Decisions

Before you make a decision, ask yourself, "Am I making this decision based on suffering or joy?"

Many people build their lives on decisions based on suffering and pain.

The way to break the pattern of going from one painful event to another is to become aware of what is motivating each choice.

Decide to make the decision based on joy rather than suffering.

You may have to pretend at first - that's okay.

Pretend you are making your decision based on joy and notice, now, all the different choices available to you.

Notice when you act from a place of joy that it *feels good* to make decisions.

When you choose from a place of suffering, you are making *victim* choices.

When you choose from a state of joy, you are making *empowered* choices.

Use your imagination and visualize all the possible choices you could make if you were basing your decisions on joy and strength.

From this moment, continue to choose from joy.

Why would you choose any other way?

~ ~ ~

Inner Time and Outer Life

Every moment of your inner time that is spent in anger, resentment or remorse is a moment wasted.

Your inner time is your greatest asset because how you spend it determines your outer life.

If your inner time is spent in turmoil, your outer life will be a reflection of that turmoil.

Where are your thoughts?

Where have they *gone*?

Are they not *within you* all along?

If they are within you, what controls them?

When you become aware of *where* your thoughts are, and *what* they are *doing*, then you have become aware of *how* you spend your inner time.

It is through this awareness that you gain control of your inner life - and, therefore, your outer life.

As this awareness increases, you learn how to *invest* your thoughts.

You learn to dismiss the unimportant, trivial, negative thoughts, and to nourish the profound, loving, positive thoughts.

Learn to invest your inner time in love, and watch it multiply into your outer life.

Don't *waste* your inner time!

Sanctuary

Deep within you is a sanctuary just waiting to be explored.

That inner holy place contains your connection to all that is sacred, strong, and serene.

When you strengthen your connection to this sanctuary and begin seeing your life from this holy point, all your troubles and suffering are subdued.

It's not that your troubles and sufferings go away; it's that they become more easily managed, more easily faced.

Trying to escape your hurts will never be successful, but as you learn to see them from a higher perspective, you have the courage to live in grace in spite of them.

This courage exists in your sanctuary.

The more you tap into this holy place, the easier it is to manifest these sacred qualities.

What else exists in this inner treasure house?

This is the place within you that is fearless!

Go there now!

Feel the strength.

Make it stronger.

From this fearless place, you can do anything; you can access all your divine qualities.

What else do you have in you inner sanctuary?

The more you access this holy place, the more you manifest these inner treasures.

Explore your heaven within - and manifest miracles!

Tiny Pleasures

Each tiny pleasure in life is to be nourished.

Each glint of sunshine on an emerald leaf is a treasure.

Each thought of joy can be multiplied into a thousand scenarios of bliss.

As you appreciate each ray of light, each growing leaf, each joyful thought, you create a world of delight.

This world begins with you and extends outwards, touching the lives around you simply because *you exist.*

The pleasures naturally express through you as you cultivate them.

Each smile you give lightens up your life and all those around you.

A smile nourishes the ecstasy within you and outside of you.

Tiny pleasures add up to the sum of your life.

They multiply and become the essence of how you create your world.

What are your tiny pleasures?

How do you nourish them?

How do you multiply them into your world?

How do you allow your treasures to influence others?

Nourish each tiny pleasure and create paradise!

ର ର ର

Allow the Light to Shine Through You

Your job is not *to be* the light, but to let the light shine *through you*.

You limit your ability to be a transmitter of this light by thinking that it *is you* doing this.

As you let go of your fears, you can become a clear channel of heavenly light to help others.

What are your fears?

Deep down you may be afraid of *yourself.*

You may be afraid you will make the wrong choice or do the wrong thing.

You may think that deep down there is evil inside you.

Because of these fears you may think you cannot be a messenger of divine energy.

Remember that these fears exist in *this earthly realm* because this is the *realm of duality.*

Don't try to banish the fears, because that gives them power.

Simply acknowledge them, and know your fears are *not you!*

Allow the light to flow through you, and the fears will vanish.

Allow the light to shine through you, and become a channel of divine energy.

Love Never Diminishes You

Your love is never wasted, nor is it in vain.

Your love has extreme value even when you think it's not returned.

The love you *give* strengthens *you*.

Giving love is a *requirement* for receiving love.

You cannot receive love until you have made room by giving it away.

Your heart breaks when you think you have to *stop* loving.

When you try to stop the flow of love, it backs up in your heart until it can no longer contain it, and then it bursts.

It's trying to *stop* the flow that causes your heart to break!

You *can't* stop loving, so you might as well not even try.

When you see the greater picture, you realize that the other person doesn't need to return your love in order for you to receive.

Your love *automatically* returns to you.

That's why the more you love, the more you *can love*.

Choose to love, regardless of the perceived outcome.

Choose to love, and *know* it comes back to you.

Your First Thought of the Day

Ask God to give you your first thought upon awakening each day.

What do you think God will give you?

Do you think God will give you thoughts of peace, love, and abundance?

Or do you think God will give you thoughts of anger, fear, and poverty?

Let's say you're pondering a situation in your life.

Before you go to sleep at night, ask God to help guide your decision by putting guidance in your first thought as you wake up in the morning.

Allow yourself to receive this thought, and say, "Thank you."

When you receive the thought, don't judge it.

Even if it doesn't make sense to you on a conscious level, don't analyze it.

Simply thank God for providing you with the thought about your situation, and let it unfold and develop throughout your day.

Continue this process and you'll find that the Divine is working in your life in fabulous ways that you could not have imagined before.

You'll begin to trust.

Your limitations will become the pathways to solutions.

Simply ask God to give you your first thought each day.

Stillness Isn't Just Stillness

Sometimes stillness is experienced in different ways.

How is this possible?

Isn't stillness just stillness?

You experience stillness differently because you continue to move up the continuum of spiritual evolution.

As you change, you experience that point of stillness from a different perspective.

That's why it's important to live in the now.

That's why time is immeasurable - because it moves inward as much as it moves outward.

Infinity occupies just as much inner time as outer time.

There is no place in time that stillness is not.

You always have access to stillness, regardless of what's going on outside of you.

As with everything, the more you practice, the easier it gets.

The more you practice accessing stillness, the more different elements of it you are able to experience.

Experiencing stillness allows you to expand time, the element in which movement takes place.

That's why each time you experience stillness; it's different.

Developing Your Soul

Begin to see all circumstances in your life as if they were specifically designed to help develop your soul.

Ask yourself, "How is this situation helping me strengthen my integrity?"

How is it helping me learn to love?

How is it helping me learn to appreciate being alive?

How is it helping me teach?

You are always learning and always teaching.

The sooner you begin to see these truths, the easier it is to learn, and the more effective you become as a teacher.

One of the things you can teach others is that one doesn't always have to learn through negativity.

Do you think that all lessons must be based on negative circumstances?

You can also learn through joy, and that is a great lesson in itself.

Remember as a child when you learned through play?

Remember one of those, "Ah-ha!" moments?

Remember the joy you felt as you had those experiences?

Now ask divine energy to allow *more* of those moments to come into your life.

Ask to learn and teach others through joy.

Then *pay attention* to all the joyful moments in your life through which you are learning.

Your soul is developing anyway; it might as well develop through joy!

Are You Thinking From a Conclusion?

Ever think ahead into the future about what might happen, and then behave as if it already has?

This is called, "Thinking from a conclusion," and it's something everyone does from time to time.

If you're thinking about something negative that may happen, you're wasting energy.

Thinking from a negative conclusion prevents the natural unfolding of positive events.

It scatters your energies and attracts negative results into your life.

As you catch yourself in this distorted realm of confused thinking, it's important to pull your energies into the present.

Ask, "Where am I now?"

Where are my energies at this moment?

Get your power back into the here and now.

Allow yourself to become balanced again.

Feel your energies become aligned with your personal power, the power of the earth, and the power of the Divine.

This is a *holy trinity.*

When you think of the future, think positive, uplifting thoughts.

Positive thoughts create positive energy.

Negative thoughts deplete energy.

As you think about the future, think about the future you would *like to create*, not about what you fear may happen.

Your thoughts help make the future a reality, so if you're thinking from a conclusion, make sure it's a positive one.

☙ ☙ ☙

Surrender

Who is in control of your life?

Who is making the decisions about how your life unfolds?

Upon what is your identity based?

To whom do you turn for guidance?

As you come to realize that you are not alone in this life, everything changes.

As you realize that you have helpers on the other side, your life opens to dramatic transformation.

As you remember that you have *soul energy* on the other side that you can *connect with now,* your entire life changes.

Who wouldn't be afraid if they thought they were alone in this world?

Thinking you are alone is akin to thinking that God has abandoned you!

God could never abandon you because you are *a part* of God!

When you make the conscious decision to allow God to control your life, everything will become blissfully easy.

It won't stay that way, of course, because you are here to experience duality, but the bliss is there when you remember to access it.

Surrender your life to the Divine and watch heaven unfold on earth.

ॐ ॐ ॐ

Trusting God

Trusting God to run your life doesn't mean that you sit back and don't make a move until you get directions from heaven.

It means you live courageously in the moment, making decisions knowing that you are doing your best.

Trusting God doesn't mean that you won't have fear; it means that you'll have the strength to move *through fear*.

Without fear you wouldn't *need* to align your energies in love.

When you align your energies in love, you align your energies in God.

Living in God's energy reminds you to be aware; reminds you of who you really are; and reminds you that you have the *forces of the universe* behind you!

How could you then lack courage?

Living in love allows your energies to align so that God's grace can flow through you.

Do you think God makes mistakes?

Do you think there are limits to infinite, divine power?

Then why would you trust your life to anything less than holy grace?

❦ ❦ ❦

Your True Identity

With what do you identify?

Do you identify with your job, your income, your gender, your house, your country, your music, your clothes, or your car?

Make a list of all the things that make you feel good, that bring you peace.

Now ask yourself what you would identify with if all those "things" were taken away from you.

Would you still feel good and have peace if you no longer had those "things" on your list?

Could you still have peace and goodness without those things?

What would you be able to access inside of yourself that would allow you to experience knowing *who you really are?*

What would you access inside yourself that would allow you to experience peace and happiness?

As you learn to access these inner states of being, you begin to experience your soul.

That is your true identity.

∽ ∽ ∽

The Highest Form of Prayer

Prayer is simply a method of directing your energy.

Prayer is a way of deliberately directing your energies into higher frequencies.

As you put your attention on these, you raise your own energies.

That's why prayer has been utilized as a pathway to the mystical world for centuries.

The ancients knew how important prayer was as a way of achieving union with the Divine.

The question is: What *kind* of prayer?

Prayers of supplication?

Prayers of gratitude?

Prayers of honor?

What kind of prayer will strengthen your bond with God?

The most powerful prayers are prayers of love.

When you ask for nothing, when you want nothing, when you allow yourself to send the pure energy of love to your creator, your entire energy field is raised to a new level.

There are no other requirements.

Love God consciously.

Make the decision to love God.

Loving God is the highest form of prayer possible.

Simply say, "I love you, God!"

Use it as a mantra.

Let it be your first waking thought - pun intended.

Living Through Sorrows

There may be times when you don't know who you are, as if you are on the verge of non-existence.

There may be times when your suffering is so great that you feel as if death is the only solution.

You must live through these sorrows.

Remember that we all face tragedy; we all face loss; we all face devastation.

Every human will experience heartbreaks.

You need to know that whatever heartbreak you experience and regardless of how you feel at the time, you are never alone.

Your angels and your heavenly guides are here to help you.

You must remember that your reactions to those difficult moments *teach those around you* how to react.

That knowledge can give you strength.

Your own loving kindness grows stronger as you develop poise through those awful times.

Become still through the sadness.

It's okay not to know.

It's okay to feel nothing.

Allow yourself to experience the emptiness of grief.

It is through emptiness that you can be filled again.

༄ ༄ ༄

True Self-Confidence

Self-confidence is simply being connected, on a deep, inner level, to unlimited, unconditional, universal love.

This love has no limits because it is not affected by your perceived deficiencies.

It is unlimited because it's unconditional.

It is *within you now,* at this very moment.

Your job is to connect with this internal divine energy and allow it to flow freely through you.

Begin by finding a tiny point of joy inside yourself.

Simply become aware of your inner place of happiness.

Now cultivate this inner place of bliss.

Allow this inner point of joy to radiate from you.

Notice how good it feels to be you, now, in this moment, as you connect with your infinite, inner joy.

Notice that from this connection to divine energy, all those perceived deficiencies you thought you had, become invitations to develop even more unconditional love.

Experience how good it feels to be totally filled with unlimited acceptance.

Having access to this now, and knowing how to regain this access at any time, you can choose to feel the self-confidence of being connected to divine love.

Self-confidence is *knowing* that you are connected to God, and always will be.

Self-confidence is really God-confidence!

෨෨ ෨෨ ෨෨

Your Job is Not to Judge

Do not let *outward* appearances dictate your *inner* reality.

A flashy smile can cover-up a broken heart.

Outward opulence can conceal inner poverty.

As you let go of judging outer events, it becomes easier to focus on inner resources.

As you begin to appreciate your body for being the vehicle of your spirit, you begin to see beauty in a new way.

As you begin to develop your inner life, your outer life becomes much more miraculous.

When you begin seeing through the eyes of love, all you witness takes on a new glory.

If you limit your vision to the exterior shell of existence, you limit your perceptions to the false gods before you.

Your job is not to judge.

Your job is to love.

The more you love, the more lovely the reality you create.

Begin with your thoughts.

Choose love.

Choose to love even if, at first, you don't feel it.

Love is a decision.

As you decide to love, you will create the reality of your dreams.

As you decide to love, you will let go of judging outward appearances.

ᘒ ᘒ ᘒ

When You Are Upset, Remember Peace

What does it mean to be upset?

Become aware of how your energy changes when you become upset.

Notice how the movement of energy changes in your body and mind as you jolt out of your center of balance.

Where does this movement occur first?

It is important to become aware of these energetic shifts so that you can manage them more easily.

If you're not aware of what happens when you're not connected to your divine nature, you become a victim of outside circumstances.

Of course, there will always be times when you are pulled out of your center of balance.

Your job is to realign your energies as soon as possible.

Do this by remembering *who you really are.*

When something upsetting happens, remember that you are a creation of God, loved on all levels of your being.

Remember that who you really are can *never be harmed* in any way.

Your body may be injured, your feelings may be hurt, but you, as a spiritual being, cannot be harmed or destroyed.

You are eternal, living forever in the arms of God, centered in holy love, full of joy and incapable of being upset.

Being upset means you have forgotten who you are.

Remember your divine nature - and return to peace.

Time is Here For You

What is time?

Time is the medium that allows you to become *conscious* in this realm.

That is the only reason time is important.

Time is a gauge.

How long will it take you to become aware of who you are and what you are doing here?

The paradox is that it doesn't matter!

You have all the time it takes.

There is *no hurry.*

Hurry implies there is *not enough* time.

Time is here *for you* to experience the beauty of unfolding.

That is why each moment is blessed: It exists *for you.*

As you appreciate each moment, it unfolds into its own world of exquisite beauty, never to exist again.

That is why appreciating each moment is vital.

Time is the most precious commodity in this realm, and yet the most undervalued.

How are you spending your time?

ை ை ை

Learning Not to Limit Love

If you limit your love, you limit yourself.

You never need to stop loving anyone, regardless of their past deeds or yours.

Trying to stop loving is futile.

It is always appropriate to love.

As you love, you hold another being in high esteem.

This helps them to express more of their potential, and also helps you to express more of yours.

Love tempers your thoughts.

Love strengthens every energy system, both inside and outside of you.

There is no power stronger than love.

Allow everything your eyes can see to become an object of your love.

Let every sound your ears can hear be a recipient of your love.

Let every object your body touches be a vessel for your love.

Put love into everything your senses can behold.

Now allow your love to transcend those things and fill the space as far as your thoughts can stretch.

By not limiting your love you set yourself *free*.

As you allow your love to grow, you allow your soul to grow.

Clarity in Confusion

Sometimes when you are in the middle of confusion, the only thing you can do to receive clarity is ask for guidance.

You can ask for a sign from your angels, and then simply be aware so that you don't overlook it.

Sometimes you are thrust out of your comfort zone and into confusion because you're being nudged by higher energies to operate on a new level.

Notice how confusion distorts your energy.

Notice how it forces you to find a new point of calmness within.

Confusion requires you to seek a deeper level of balance.

Confusion forces you to re-evaluate your position in the universe.

Confusion is a sign of growth in itself.

Don't condemn confusion; embrace it!

Confusion means you are ready to advance.

Whatever happens is for your betterment.

It is okay not to know.

As you accept confusion, guidance is easier to receive.

It's part of the paradox of being human.

Accept confusion so that you can receive clarity on a new level.

૭ ૭ ૭

Inner and Outer Directedness

There are times when you are inner directed, and times when you are outer directed.

When you are inner directed, your perceptions revolve around how you feel, how you think, and your own individual activities.

When you are outer directed, your perceptions involve what others are doing and circumstances in the outer world.

Both inward focus and outward focus are necessary.

Simply notice how the energy shifts when you change your focus.

Notice what energy centers are activated as you change your attention from inside yourself to outside yourself.

Your development depends upon how *you manage your energy*.

The first step in learning to manage this energy is to become aware of it.

Notice that as you become aware of the energy, *it changes!*

Your very awareness has the power to *change energy*.

That's a lot of power!

That's why, as your awareness grows, *your power grows*, in both inward and outward directions!

Overcoming Doubt

One of the biggest lessons you get to learn in life is overcoming doubt.

It is not uncommon to doubt who you are.

You might doubt your decision-making abilities, your talents, your skills, or your creativity.

You might even look to others for reassurance.

But as you develop your ability to connect with divine energy, you develop your ability to trust the Divine within.

Become familiar with the quiet.

Seek the stillness within.

Within the inner stillness is the vortex that draws all wisdom to you.

This is the gateway from one realm of consciousness to another.

This is the point on the path of infinity in which you truly exist.

This is your place of power, peace, and transformation, where you are able to experience oneness with all.

There is no doubt here, because there is no duality here.

Timeless, stillness, infinite, now!

This is the perfect moment and the perfect place, where you are now!

You are its masterpiece.

How can you doubt that, now?

∾ ∾ ∾

Let Yourself Love Beyond Measure

Who you love is not important; what matters is simply that *you love.*

You may need an object, someone or something outside yourself to which you can direct your love.

This external object serves as a teacher.

If it returns your love, you feel safe and secure and continue to let your love flow.

If the external object does not return your love, you may feel injured and hurt.

Once you learn that it's not important who or what you love, you can extend and widen your focus so that your love is inclusive and unconditional.

Experience how good it feels, just for a moment, to send your love out to include all people, all animals, all places, all things.

Do it just for a moment.

Notice that nothing can *contain* your love.

That's what the scripture, "My cup runneth over," means.

You have the capacity to love beyond measure.

As you exercise this capacity, you become a beacon of light for the entire world.

Let yourself love.

Let yourself *love!*

૦૦ ૦૦ ૦૦

Loving Your Enemy Isn't For Your Enemy

Jesus said to love your enemy for a reason - and it *wasn't* to benefit your enemy.

Having an enemy in the first place implies having malice in your heart.

You can't have malice and love in your heart at the same time.

Keeping anything but love in your heart is simply a waste of time and energy.

Every moment you spend on negative thoughts is one less moment you spend in love.

When you find it too difficult to shift your energy to love, call on the Holy Spirit to do it for you.

The Holy Spirit does for you what you, a mere human, find impossible.

Sometimes the best you can do is give your anger to the Holy Spirit.

Invite the Holy Spirit to remove the negativities in your heart and replace them with love.

The message is just as important now as it was two thousand years ago.

Don't clog your heart with hatred.

You're the only one who feels what's in your heart!

That's why it's important to love your enemy!

∾ ∾ ∾

Sarcasm Only Works in Sitcoms

Sarcasm works in sitcoms because the characters aren't real and don't have to recover from hurt feelings.

A question is, "Why am I entertained when someone else gets his or her feelings hurt?"

Why does another's embarrassment cause you to laugh?

When you try to use television tactics in real life, it backfires.

You really don't want to be *laughed at,* and you really don't want to be embarrassed in front of your friends, so why would putting others in those positions be acceptable?

Sarcasm is really a cover-up for what you really want: Love and acceptance.

Sarcasm creates distance and a false sense of superiority that the fearful think they need in order to be safe.

Attacking others never results in safety.

Safety is a natural side effect of identifying with who you really are: A divine, holy creation of infinite love.

There is no need for sarcasm when you identify with your own inner sanctity.

Let the TV characters take care of themselves; they're not real anyway!

Write the script for your life from your heart - where purity, integrity, joy, and delight exist.

∾ ∾ ∾

314

Gentleness and Strength

Developing gentleness is as important as developing strength.

In fact, true gentleness requires strength to develop.

The weak cannot be gentle because they're terrified.

The meek shall inherit the earth because only the gentle have true strength.

How gentle can you be?

How strong can you be?

All you need is the strength to say, "yes" or "no."

"Yes" and "no" empower you to use free will.

When you are afraid you can't make the decision to say "yes" or "no" wisely.

When you are not afraid you are empowered with love, calmness, strength, and gentleness.

Feel the difference.

Breathe in the gentleness of love and feel your strength.

Stand on the earth and let its quiet power flow through you.

Let your own strength develop as you make peace within.

Be gentle.

Feel your strength.

Adoration

Many *seek* adoration, yet don't know *how* to adore.

You may want to *be* loved, yet may *withhold* your love from others.

Loving is not a game.

Loving is life itself!

Loving another cannot hurt you.

You are hurt when your expectations of another's behavior are not fulfilled.

What if you gave yourself permission to have no expectations?

Do you have expectations of a flower?

Do you have expectations of a newborn?

Feel the difference in your body when you make the decision *not* to love that flower or that newborn child.

Experience the inner light dimming as you withhold love.

Now let yourself love again!

Feel the relief, the freedom, the lightness of allowing yourself to be who you really are: A light beam of divine love.

When you make the decision not to love, you cut yourself off from the creative flow of the universe.

You don't *need* to be adored by another.

You experience adoration as you *allow yourself* to adore, to freely love – period!

ᘓ ᘓ ᘓ

Suicide

When you destroy your own physical life, you give permission to those around you to *destroy theirs*.

Suicide has a profound, rippling effect on all humans.

You cannot commit suicide and take *only* your own life.

People want to kill themselves because they think death will end their suffering.

Death simply removes the physical vehicle through which suffering could have been *processed*.

Suicide leaves those still in the physical realm filled with guilt and grief.

We are not taught *how* to die.

We are not taught the art of easing our consciousness out of our bodies when the time comes to leave earth.

We are taught to hold on, to fight, to demand more time!

There is no point in hanging on if you haven't developed the ability to *let go*.

As you learn to *value the time* you spend *in* your body, it will become easier to ease out of it.

If you want to end suffering, work on *transformation*, and the body will take care of itself.

Love and Relationships

Don't feel bad about being duped in love.
All have had first impressions backfire.
Some relationships are not meant to grow.
Sometimes you learn more by *not* having a certain relationship develop.
The hopes that you had for the failed relationship will unfold, but in a different, more mature way, in a future relationship.
Love is never lost.
Love is never wasted.
Let the love flow from your heart.
Don't try to hold it back or your heart will break.
Don't limit love's path or it won't come back to you.
There is no need for you to decide whom your love touches and whom it does not.
True love does not discriminate.
When you limit your love, you limit yourself.
Don't worry about being duped.
Let the love flow and it will come back and bless you.

෨ ෨ ෨

How You Influence The Universe

Your life is so intricately intertwined with all other lives that you *can't help* but influence others.

You are a force in this universe whether you know it or not.

Be aware of it!

Know it!

Feel it!

You have within you the most powerful energy in the universe: The force of life itself!

You would not be able to read or hear these words unless you were powered by life!

Let yourself feel the privilege of existing in a three-dimensional body on this planet!

Feel the life force beating your heart, breathing your lungs, and connecting you to the earth.

Let yourself feel the effervescence found only in these realms.

Feel the energy that is uniquely you!

Ask, "What is the most compelling force in my life?"

Open your heart and listen.

Become aware of who you are on a deep, inner level.

Become aware of *how* you are influencing others.

The only energy you can truly transform is your own.

As you become aware of your energy, you can better choose how you'd like to use it, and how *you'd like* to influence the universe.

Optimal Times, Optimal Outcomes

When you have trouble accomplishing a task, change the time of day you would normally try to accomplish it.

Timing affects everything.

There are times when the energy flows more easily, so it's easier to accomplish certain goals.

These times of efficient energy flow are both individual and universal.

Neither time nor energy is stagnant.

Not one atom stays the same for one moment.

There is constant, unique change occurring at all times.

Each form of energy has its optimal time for expression.

You wouldn't expect a sunset to occur at dawn.

A plant produces seed only when it's ready.

High tide and low tide occur on schedule.

Some goals cannot be rushed.

Sometimes the process needs to be shifted through time in order to manifest the outcome.

Simply changing the time changes the process.

Experiment.

Find the optimal time to achieve a task and you'll achieve the optimal outcome.

∽ ∽ ∽

Your Real Powers

Become aware of your deepest, innermost desires.

You must become aware of them in order to fulfill or discard them.

If you are not aware, they will rule your life anyway, only without your control or consent.

In order to say *No,* you must know to what you are saying *No*.

In order to say *Yes,* you must know to what you are saying *Yes*.

Yes and *No* are your only *real powers.*

You are saying *Yes* or *No* all the time, you simply aren't aware of it.

Yes and No, choices made consciously, become a *sacred sacrament.*

As you begin to consciously choose, your whole life reflects the holiness of your choices.

Your life takes on an intention, a focus, which allows you to fulfill your purpose with ease and comfort.

Choice is your real power!

To what are you saying *Yes* and *No*?

❧ ❧ ❧

Letting Go Of Resentment

Resentments are the result of expectations not being met, little disappointments that you keep alive by remembering them.

Resentments may involve another person, but the most difficult ones to let go of involve you.

Have you ever resented yourself?

There may be a place deep inside of you that is seething with disappointment and remorse about your own behavior.

What is in your past that you'd like to change?

What would you have done differently?

When you are able to go deep inside and forgive yourself for not living up to your own expectations, you will be able to forgive others more easily.

Forgiveness of self is the underlying requirement for letting go of resentment.

Feeling the pain again doesn't make it better; it makes it worse.

Every time you experience resentment, the negativity rut gets deeper and deeper.

Bless yourself.

Bless yourself and there will be no room for negativity.

Let the blessings fill the ruts and resentment won't have a chance to create a foothold.

Bless yourself and let go of the resentments.

ॐ ॐ ॐ

How to Modify Pain

If you live long enough in the body, you will experience physical pain.

The first step in dealing with pain is to recognize that it is your body's pain, *not your pain.*

This recognition requires the realization that you are *not* your body!

This realization allows you to experience pain without emotional discomfort.

You can then experience pain as simply energy in the body.

This energy can be intense or it can be dull.

It can be steady or it can be throbbing.

It can be warm or it can be cold.

The more specifically you can identify the energy, the more removed you can become from it.

This energy in your body is *not you.*

You can alter how you experience this energy by how you perceive it.

You do not have to be its victim.

You have the ability to modify your perceptions.

Your perceptions determine your experience.

Your *reaction* to the pain is what *you experience.*

Change how you react and you change the experience.

As you change the experience, you change the pain.

Next time you have a pain, ask yourself what you are experiencing and how you would like to *change* that experience!

The Life of Your Dreams

Don't let circumstances dictate how you feel, or you will always be a victim.

If you let poverty, ill health, or poor relationships determine how you are feeling and what you are thinking at any given moment, then you will never be in control of your *self*.

You must learn to tap into the power, the joy, the love and the bliss that lie within you, regardless of external circumstances.

As you learn this, your outer circumstances will naturally change to reflect these treasures.

As you begin developing your inner resources, your outer resources will grow.

How do you *want to feel?*

Allow yourself to feel that now, this instant, this moment.

Notice that as your feelings and your thinking come together, your body begins to reflect this unity.

As you learn to align your energies from within, you begin to understand how ludicrous it is to let outer circumstances dictate your state of being.

You are deciding your inner state moment-by-moment, thought-by-thought, and feeling-by-feeling.

Create the life of your dreams, one thought, one feeling, and one action at a time!

ல ல ல

Bring Joy to the World

The ability to experience joy is determined by your inner capacity to feel bliss, not by your outer circumstances.

Nothing has the ability to *make* you happy.

That job is entirely up to you.

If you could *feel* any way you wanted, how would you feel?

If you could *think* any way you wanted, how would you think?

If you could *be* any way you wanted, how would you *be?*

Decide how you want to be and then cultivate all your energies so they help you flow in that direction.

Do not be swayed by outside circumstances.

They will naturally begin to reflect the new direction of your energy flow in due time.

Your job is to develop your *inner* resources so that no matter what happens, you have access to peace.

Inner peace is the true meaning of independence and liberation.

Whatever you cultivate within will naturally express itself in the outer world.

Creation always begins on the inside.

That's why joy is determined by your ability to create it.

Don't wait for the world to bring you joy.

Bring joy to the world.

෴ ෴ ෴

Stop Trying

What is it that you are *trying* to experience?

Whatever it is, stop it, immediately.

You cannot have a true, pure experience, if *trying* is involved.

Feel the difference in your body as you give up trying.

Trying requires tension.

Peace requires *letting go* of tension.

You cannot experience peace and oneness through trying.

Trying only works when you want to achieve an outer goal, like building a house, or riding a bicycle.

Most people associate not trying with giving up or self-sabotage, but that's not what it means at all.

Self-sabotage is giving up on yourself, defeating yourself, fighting yourself.

Not trying is like giving up the fight so that peace can flow through you.

Your natural energy flow is totally peaceful.

This flow gets contaminated with expectations and demands you make on yourself and others.

That is the true meaning of *desire*.

That's why the sages urge you to give up your desires.

When you give up the war of trying, you free yourself to experience your natural state: Bliss!

You can't *try* to experience bliss; you *allow* yourself to experience it.

What would you like to *allow* yourself to experience?

ᖡ ᖡ ᖡ

The Night and Rain of the Soul

Grief is not to be minimized.

You may know intellectually that you will be reunited with your loved ones, but that doesn't lessen sorrow when they are no longer in this earthly realm.

Sadness cannot be overcome; it must be lived through.

You don't get rid of grief; you learn how to live with it.

If you haven't experienced that hollow, empty, abysmal loss, it's because you haven't experienced it, *yet*.

Don't try to eliminate grief.

Ask what it *wants* for you.

Does grief want you to stop loving?

Of course not.

Grief may want you to love *more*.

Grief may want you to honor your beloved.

Grief may want you to honor the love your beloved has *for you*.

Loving doesn't mean living pain-free.

Loving means living through pain and continuing to love anyway.

You don't need to let go of grief.

Grief will *let go of you* as you *continue to love*.

Allow yourself to love, no matter what, and grief will lessen its hold on you.

Roses require the darkness of night and the dampness of rain to grow.

Grief is the night and the rain of the soul.

Don't minimize it.

Grow through it.

A Life With No Regrets

The biggest regret that you will ever have is withholding love.

Withholding love constricts the flow of energy into all of your systems: Spiritual, emotional, mental, and physical.

Experience the sensations when you make the decision to stop loving.

Feel the tightness and constrictions that develop in your body, your emotions, and your thoughts.

Notice how shut down you feel: Closed off and isolated.

Now *allow yourself to love.*

Let the expansion occur on all levels of your being as you allow the love to flow through all your systems.

Feel the freedom of opening your heart to love.

Just love!

As you love, you open your heart to the miracle of creation.

As you love, you open your heart to more love.

Feel the strength in deciding to love.

There is no stronger power in the universe!

Let yourself be the center through which love flows.

Live a life of no regrets - let yourself love!

Your True Nature Is Joy

Think of joy as golden drops of liquid gently falling on the top of your head.

These gentle drops of joy have the ability to permeate your skin and enter into your bloodstream.

They fill your entire body with delight, comfort, and bliss.

Feel the energy as it sparkles with ecstasy throughout your entire being.

Allow yourself to feel the freedom of receiving bliss.

This ecstasy is the creative energy of the universe, otherwise known as love.

As you learn to identify with this natural creative force, you learn to identify with your true, inner nature.

You already have the exquisite nature of joy within, or you wouldn't be able to recognize it.

Honor it and it will grow.

Experience the bliss of who you are, now, this moment!

This is your *true nature!*

This joy is underneath all the blocks, all the anger, all the anxiety, all the depression, all the grief, and all the jealousy that you may ever experience.

If you haven't been experiencing joy, it's because you've been identifying with your *false nature.*

Identify with your true nature and feel the golden drops of joy within.

"Controlling" Anger

What "makes" you angry?

Whatever causes you to be angry has more power than you do.

Don't try *not* to be angry; that's just sending your energy down the same wasted path.

Recognize what makes you angry and ask yourself, "Why?"

What angers you, threatens you.

Ask yourself what is within you that feels threatened.

Become aware of how your energy changes when you are angry.

Where do you feel it first?

What happens next?

It's not the *initial* anger that's harmful; it's hanging on to it.

It's perfectly natural to become angry, to become threatened.

You feel threatened when you identify with your human body.

When you remember that you are *not* your body, you can release the threat and let go of the anger.

Identify with your higher aspects and you won't feel threatened.

Identify with who *you really are* and regain your power.

Regain your power and know that nothing can *make* you angry.

Poise Under Pressure

The secret to a fabulous life is learning not to be upset when your plumbing backs up.

Can you be a mystic when your electricity goes off?

How does a serene one handle a toothache?

If you can't access tranquility during ordinary troubled times, what good is it?

The secret to poise under pressure is remembering *who you really are.*

If your body experiences a toothache, be aware that it is your *body* that has a problem, not *you!*

Your job is to *solve* the problem if you can.

If your house is having plumbing problems, ask, "What is the most efficient way I can solve this?"

Focus on *solving* the problem.

You are *not* the problem; your job is to solve the problem the best way you can.

Handle the problem without identifying with it and you will have learned the fabulous secret to poise under pressure!

∽ ∽ ∽

Beyond the Physical

See the sparkles of light dance on the leaves.
Hear the trees whisper in the wind.
Smell the softness of the earth.
Feel the warmth of the sun's kiss.
Taste the silkiness of a raindrop.

These are energies you experience through your physical body.

There are other, more subtle energies that are just as real.

These energies may be experienced through avenues other than the body's senses.

These energies are just as real, just as important, as the energies your body senses.

You may experience these energies as inner sights or inner sounds.

You may experience these energies as simply a knowing, a certainty, or a nudge.

As you *validate* your inner experiences, you allow them to become stronger.

This is a way of honoring all the aspects of who you are.

Learn to see the sparkles on the inside as well as the outside.

As your perceptions expand, your world expands!

Honor your *inner* world as well as your outer world.

When You Need Prayers

It has been said that you only appreciate prayer when you need it yourself.

True prayer is simply holding loving thoughts.

When you pray for others, see them happy and healthy, *regardless* of outer appearances.

The more you hold these positive thoughts *in mind,* the more you help bring positive aspects into the physical.

Positive thoughts help not only the person you are praying for; they help you, too, because you are *experiencing* the positive energy as you pray!

That's why true prayer is like mercy; it blesses both the giver and the receiver.

If you hold others in loving thought you are experiencing the benefits of prayer-- and they are, too!

When *you* need prayers, hold *yourself* in loving thought.

Bless yourself just as you bless others.

Be the giver and the receiver!

Surely you can bless yourself as you bless others!

Your Holy Life

Your life is holy.
Every single soul has the ability to live a sacred life.
There are no favorites in God's kingdom.
There is no hierarchy of souls on the earth plane.
God does not love anyone more than you!
Darkness and despair come from your *own* judgment and condemnation.
Unconditional love cannot discriminate.
It is the *limit* you put on your ability to love that causes you pain; nothing else can.
As you let yourself love freely, you experience the holiness of your being.
Love.
Experience your holiness.
There is no one God loves more than you!

You *Can't* Stop Loving

You are never vulnerable when you love.

When you arm yourself with love you cannot be wounded.

True love cannot hurt or be hurt.

Loving is part of your true nature, and when you love, you experience more of who you really are.

You become vulnerable when you try to *stop* the flow of love, or when you try to limit the flow to one particular person, place or thing.

Love cannot be limited.

Love has no limits.

The pain associated with love doesn't result from loving; it results from *trying* to *stop loving*.

Who do you hurt when you make the decision to withhold your love?

Where does that love go when you *try* to stop it?

You can't stop yourself from loving.

It simply doesn't work.

You can't stop the most powerful force in the universe.

True, unconditional love cannot hurt because it doesn't exist on the level of duality, where pain is felt.

Allowing yourself to love unconditionally, in total freedom, raises your consciousness to a higher level, a level beyond pain.

That's why you are *not* vulnerable when you love!

Releasing Jealousy

There is no reason to ever feel jealous.

Others' gifts are merely a reflection of your own.

You are not diminished by another's greatness; you are enhanced by it!

You have within an endless pool of resources.

It's up to you to tap into this infinite pool of riches.

Jealousy emerges from the belief in competition.

Competition emerges from the belief in warfare.

Warfare emerges from the belief in lack.

Lack is based in fear.

Of what are you afraid?

Jealousy is simply another manifestation of fear.

There is *no one more holy* than *you.*

When you recognize your own holiness, you will naturally let go of fear and all its manifestations.

As you learn to *accept* God's love, God's love is what you will manifest in your life.

Fear cannot exist in the presence of love.

The freedom that you have when you accept your holiness immerses you in the divine pool of infinite treasures.

How could you ever be jealous when all on heaven and earth is *yours?*

❧ ❧ ❧

Death is the Soul's Liberation

There is no need to fear death.

Would you fear the welcoming arms of your beloved?

It serves no purpose to cling to tired, worn-out bodies when a celebration of welcome awaits you on the other side.

There is no pain at the moment of your heavenly transition; rather, there is a blessed peace that cannot be duplicated on this earthly plane.

Death is only a loss for those remaining in the earthly realm.

The sense of loss is lessened if you focus on your loved one's gain.

Death seems like "the end," because of the body's destruction, but the body's destruction is the soul's liberation.

Think of your loved one, liberated, free, transcending all of earth's ills!

Focus on the extreme bliss the soul experiences on this ever-upward journey.

Death is not a sentence: It is a celebration!

The earth cries and heaven rejoices!

Of course, tears are natural - but turn them into tears of joy and celebrate this holy transition with heaven.

The greatest gift you can give to those making this awesome journey is your blessing.

As you do so, you add to the sense of freedom and joy.

This is giving a true gift.

Do not fear death; seek to understand it.

Oneness

We are one.

That is why, even though we exist as separate beings, we have the ability to recognize the same truth.

The truth exists as an internal standard in each of us because we are all connected.

Just as the human body is one entity, yet has distinct parts, you exist in the body of God, yet separately.

Whatever your eyes experience affects your heart.

Whatever your heart experiences affects your brain.

Whatever your brain experiences affects everything.

Everything affects everything.

Just because you can't see the connections doesn't mean they are not there.

This is written to help you remember your wholeness.

This is written to help you strengthen your connection to your inner core so that you can access your own wisdom.

This *is* your own wisdom!

What is wise in me is wise in you.

Your thoughts occur in my mind.

I suffer with your sorrows.

Your wisdom brings me comfort.

We are one.

Your Inner Sanctum

Ask a question.

Sit quietly.

Go deep inside and let the answer come to you.

Honor the information you receive.

You may not understand it at first, but honor it.

Go deeper into the silence.

Allow more information to emerge.

Keep going deeper until there are no more questions.

Keep going deeper until there are no more answers.

With practice, you will enter the stillness where all information exists.

In this space of stillness, there are no more questions, because *you are one* with all knowledge.

There are no questions, because there is no uncertainty.

This place of stillness is available to all, because it is inside all who seek.

This inner sanctum is where all souls connect.

It is not so much your question that leads to this inner, holy place; it is the *honor* you give the answer.

Ask.

Sit.

Receive.

Honor.

Practice.

Centering in God's Energy

What helps you balance?

What do you need to do each day to help you live from the center of your God-being?

It is important, before you begin your associations with the outer world, to establish yourself firmly in your inner world of the Divine.

You will not be pleased with your life until you establish yourself as a living conduit for divine energy.

When your earthly energies are balanced, heavenly energies can flow through you.

That is when you fulfill your destiny and become an open channel for divine love.

If you are not letting God use you as His instrument, you will feel emptiness or yearning inside you.

God cannot use you until you give up using yourself.

There can be only one driver in each vehicle.

Surrender yourself to divine love and let God be your driver.

Ask what you can do each day to center yourself in God's energy.

There are no insignificant thoughts or deeds.

Find balance and you will become a channel for God's love in every thought and every deed in your life.

Your Holiness Needs No Proof

There is no need for you to prove yourself to anyone.

Who you really are never needs justification.

The more you live in the space of who you really are, the more peaceful and happy you'll be.

The ego requires justification for its existence because the ego isn't real.

What is real, what is true, never needs justification.

The ego exists in a state of struggle for its very life.

The ego can't relax or it would die.

The ego exists inside constantly monitored self-imposed boundaries.

The real you has no boundaries.

The real you is connected to *all that is.*

The real you experiences bliss beyond the ego's imagining.

You are *naturally holy.*

When you see your own holiness, you will naturally see the holiness in others.

Holiness needs no justification.

Holiness is what is left after the falseness of the ego has been stripped away.

Let yourself be who you are - pure, holy, loving, accepting - entirely free of needing "proof."

Make Sending Blessings a Habit

Establishing routines makes it easier to accomplish your goals.

You can make a routine of sending blessings.

You are going to have habits anyway; why not make them positive and productive?

What kinds of habits do you have now, and who is benefiting from them?

You can create a routine to send blessings to the one who provokes negativity in you.

Become aware the very instant you are having a negative reaction.

Now send a blessing to whatever caused the negative reaction in you.

There are many ways to send blessings.

You may picture a beautiful light enveloping a particular person, place, or event.

You may send loving angels to watch over people.

You may simply say, "Bless you!"

However you bless is okay; you can't do it wrong!

As you make a habit to send blessings, you receive them.

Why not make it a habit to bless?

The Gift of Your Weakness

You are both fragile and strong in your own way.

Sometimes it may feel as if you have a weakness with which you can no longer cope.

You may feel overwhelmingly fragile, as if that weakness has gotten the best of you.

What is the gift underlying this weakness?

What is the gift at the end of your fragility?

Perhaps it is the gift of *surrender*.

The only way to experience true enlightenment is *surrendering to God*; that's where all weaknesses and fragilities lead, if you are wise enough to let them.

Underneath all the techniques to success, all the different schools of knowledge, all the many paths to progress, lies surrender to the Divine.

Surrendering to God's energy is the only true way your energies can align with universal energies.

With what other energy would you want alignment?

The gift of your weakness is that it reminds you of the path on which you're supposed to be: The path of divine surrender.

∽ ∽ ∽

Get Refreshed!

When you feel tired, begin to use your energy in a different way.

That's the value of going on vacation.

When you take a vacation, chances are you use *more* energy than usual.

However, because you're doing something different, it *feels* invigorating.

Even when you feel the need to "rest," you're using energy; you're just using it differently.

Being tired indicates you've been in a repetitive pattern of energy use.

That's why worry is so exhausting.

You may get into a pattern of worry, and then you're exhausted and you don't know why.

When you shift your attention to something that brings you joy rather than something that brings you fear, you become refreshed.

Ever notice when you sit all day or even lie in bed for a long time, that you're tired?

That's because you've created an energy rut.

You create an energy rut whenever you repeat the same activity or negative thought, over and over.

Interrupt the activity or thought with something totally different, and notice how much better you feel.

That's why "taking a break," is so important.

Shift your energy and get refreshed!

The Pages of God's Book

There are no blank pages in God's book.

Every single page is filled with love for you.

There has not been a time, even for one moment, when divine devotion hasn't been showered upon you.

You are continually bathed in holy grace.

As you turn your attention to the heavens, you become more aware of this ethereal energy that has been surrounding you all the time.

Breathe in the effervescence of God's love for you!

Allow yourself to fill with the joy God takes in your very existence.

Let divine bliss circulate throughout your entire being!

Feel the strength of each divine moment of awareness.

The knowledge and acceptance of God's love for you will quicken your ascent into mystical consciousness.

The path of the mystic is paved with self-love, not selfish-love.

Accepting God's love is the first step in accepting your own love for all humanity.

Love *for you* fills the pages of God's book, so that you can extend holiness to all.

෯ ෯ ෯

Endless Worlds

The wonders of the inner worlds are endless.

There are infinite inner worlds, just as there are infinite outer worlds.

No world exists independently.

When something happens in one, it affects all others.

As you develop appreciation for one realm, you develop appreciation for all.

Be gentle with your inner worlds, as you are gentle with your outer worlds.

Your entire body reacts to the inner world of your thinking.

Let yourself *feel* how your body is reacting to your thoughts.

Notice that when you have a fearful thought, your muscles tighten.

Notice that when you have a loving thought, your muscles relax.

Allowing yourself to experience loving thoughts helps soften the boundaries between the realms.

Cultivate love and allow yourself to experience endless worlds.

Cultivate loving thoughts and allow the endless wonders of your inner world to unfold!

~ ~ ~

Paranoid Thoughts

Don't feed your paranoid thoughts.
You do this by giving them your attention.
The energy investment isn't worth it.
Unless you're in the business of writing horror stories, paranoid thinking serves no purpose.

We all have paranoid thoughts; the trick is to "catch" them before they evolve into life-defeating scenarios.

As you develop awareness, you can "catch" your negative thinking and release it before it develops power over you.

Think about what you could accomplish if you could focus your thoughts *only* on achieving a certain goal.

The energy you expend on reaching any single goal begins with a *single thought*.

Ask yourself what your motivation is.

If you are motivated because you are afraid of something, your thoughts are going to be fear-based.

Regardless of your motivation, you are still subject to negative thoughts; that's why it's so important to become aware of them before they take hold of your energy.

Know that it's a blessing to be aware of your thoughts.

Only when you are *aware* of them can you make the choice to *change* them!

Don't feed your paranoid thoughts; *bless* your awareness of them so you can focus on positive, loving thoughts instead.

That's where your energy investment will really pay!

Honoring Others

How do you honor the people in your life?

One of the most effective ways you can transmit positive energy to another is through a *smile*.

Flowers are like smiles from the earth.

Stars are like smiles from the heavens.

Songs are like smiles from the heart.

We each have our own ways of smiling, and our smiles are as unique as the love in our hearts.

You honor others by extending this love.

As you do so, you create room for *more love* to enter your heart.

The more you share love, the more it grows.

The more smiles you give, the more smiles you get.

Honor another and you honor yourself.

Dishonor another and you dishonor yourself.

The honor that you give another reverberates throughout every cell in your body, and the dishonor you give another does the same.

That's why the gift of a smile works in both directions.

It is as universal as the flowers, the stars, the songs, and the smiles.

That's why it's so important to be aware of *how* you honor others in your life.

∾ ∾ ∾

Open the Door to Fantastical Realms

There are fantastical, mystical realms that exist alongside the earthly realms.

One of the secrets to becoming aware of these realms is realizing that the earthly realms aren't ordinary at all!

Once you begin to appreciate the magic of the earthly realms, the magic of the other realms becomes available to you.

The very air you breathe is filled with the magic of phantasmagoria!

Each leaf is alive with the fuel of the universe!

Your own human heart is pumped with the electricity of life itself!

The magic that exists within you is alive with joy whether you acknowledge it or not!

The *acknowledgment*, however, is the *key* to opening the portals into deeper, mystical worlds.

Acknowledgment softens the barriers your linear mind has constructed to keep you safe.

Your linear mind may fear the mystical realms because they cannot be *logically* understood.

The fear designed to keep you safe in *these* realms may prevent you from experiencing the joys of coexisting realms.

Focus on something in these realms that brings you joy.

Allow your joy to spread and it will open the doors into the bliss and wonderment of the fantastical realms.

Acknowledge, honor, and *experience!*

Reflecting the Holy Light

The holy light of your angels' vision shines down upon you.
You are always blessed with this sacred energy.

This energy is here to soothe and protect you at all times.

This holy force is more powerful than any other energy in the universe.

As you become aware of this energy, you begin reflecting it to others, just as the moon reflects the powerful light of the sun.

Don't try to hang onto the energy or capture it.

The light of your angels is to be used in *each moment*.

It is never the same, yet constant.

It is always moving, yet steady.

It is always new, yet as ancient as the universe itself.

It is as powerful as it is gentle, as strong as it is kind, and as warm as it is loving.

Let the light of your angels gleam through your eyes and shine upon all around you.

This is how *you* become a beacon of light; by reflecting the light your angels are shining upon you!

〜 〜 〜

God's Way of Speaking

God speaks to you in many ways.

God's way of speaking to you is as unique as you are.

The twinkling of a star, the chattering of a bird, the fragrance of a rose: All are messages of divine love.

Your holy task is to acknowledge these divine messages. Listen!

What worlds exist within your every breath?

What songs do you hear in the land of your dreams?

What sights do you see with your inner eye?

The messages you receive from within are just as important as those from outside.

God speaks to you in *all* your worlds.

As you increase your levels of awareness, you increase your ability to perceive in all the realms.

If you could hear God speak, what would you *want* Him to say?

Let yourself hear this message, because in truth, this is God speaking to you.

God longs for you to hear how much He loves you.

God longs for you to know that you are *already* forgiven for everything for which you have judged yourself wrong.

Let yourself accept divine love and you will hear God's messages loud and clear, or soft and sweet!

∾ ∾ ∾

Forgiveness is the Foundation

Forgiveness is the highest form of work you can do on the planet.

Forgiveness is also the *hardest* work you can do on the planet!

It is the foundation of unconditional love and requires that you breathe in the great light of humility and breathe out the darkness of judgment.

Forgiveness means you no longer perceive someone else as "wrong," and that you no longer perceive *yourself* as wrong.

You cannot judge another without judging yourself.

Judgment keeps you at the self-centered level of consciousness where suffering exists.

When you give up judgment, you give up suffering.

That's why forgiveness is so important.

Forgiveness lifts you to higher levels of consciousness.

Forgiveness doesn't exist in the lower levels.

Judgment keeps you stuck.

Start with yourself.

As you forgive yourself, you forgive others.

As you love yourself, you love others.

Forgive yourself and start loving unconditionally!

Divine Creation Exists Within You!

The beauty, the wisdom, and the glory of the heavens exist within *you*.

As you recognize these heavenly resources within, you honor yourself.

As you honor yourself, you honor *all* of divine creation!

As you progress along the mystic's path, you'll become aware that the only separation in these realms exists in your *own mind*.

Fear may exist within you because you don't trust your knowledge of these heavenly realms.

Fear results when you only access the lower realms of consciousness.

As you learn to trust the unlimited divine resources you have, fear diminishes.

You are the manifestation of a single thought of God's joy!

When you take joy in *yourself*, you take joy in God's holy creation.

Honor yourself and you honor the creator.

Divine creation is the very essence of your beauty, wisdom, and glory!

Take joy in this divine creation *now!*

Cultivating Joy

Cultivating joy is no small task.

Cultivating joy requires extreme, intense dedication.

Cultivating joy requires moment-to-moment, second-to-second devotion.

Joy is a natural result of devotion.

Devotion is simply allowing your energies to focus on love.

Allow your energies to focus on an object of love and you naturally feel joy.

Feel yourself tingling with the higher vibration of this energy.

Let yourself feel joy in the fragrance of each holy moment!

Let yourself vibrate to the sacred sounds of the universe!

Each moment is an opportunity to experience the joy of *allowing yourself to love.*

Each moment is an opportunity to radiate this joy to others.

There are infinite possibilities to experience joy.

The ability to experience joy requires only your *intention* and your *attention.*

Intend to experience joy, and then *attend* to each moment.

You are experiencing each moment anyway; it might as well be joyful!

∾ ∾ ∾

The Magnitude of a Simple Choice

Have you seen one hummingbird feather?

Have you isolated your favorite note in your favorite song?

Can you describe *exactly* the way your favorite fragrance smells?

On one hand, it doesn't seem to matter what the individual components of your life are.

On the other hand, these individual components are vital, because without each single one of them, the whole wouldn't exist.

Your whole life is comprised of seemingly insignificant components, and yet who you are is a result of all those little parts.

Some of those parts you can control and some you can't.

You can make an extreme difference in your life by changing just *one part* that is within your control.

Think, for example, what would happen if you stopped brushing your teeth.

Eventually, your teeth would decay and fall out.

In the process, it would affect your personal appearance and maybe your relationships.

Now think of how your life would be different if you decided to *look for all the joys.*

The iridescence of a single feather would dazzle you!

The glory of one note in a song would fill you with bliss.

Decide now, in one simple choice, to discover the components of joy in your life!

The Soul-ution

You may think you can't focus on joy because you're too busy focusing on the daily business of getting through life.

It is at those times, *especially*, that you need to breathe in the joy of life.

You breathe anyway, regardless of how busy you are, so you might as well breathe in joy!

Becoming aware of your breath helps you shift your attention from your worries to your joys.

Know that you can always return to your worries, but for the moment, focus on breathing in joy.

It's putting your attention on your worries that causes you to be overwhelmed.

Breathe in the calmness of the moment and let your attention focus on the 'soul'-ution instead of the problem.

Become aware that the same amount of time exists regardless of what you are doing with your energy.

Become aware that it actually takes *more energy* to be upset than it does to be calm.

The business of your daily life will always exist, interrupting you, getting in your way, and being bothersome, serving up life!

Breathe in the peace and let life have its way; it's going to anyway.

It's your job to decide how you want to exist *within* that life.

Focus on joy.

Breathe in peace.

Let your soul unfold.

Judgment and Forgiveness

Forgiveness does not require *doing* something.
It requires *undoing* something: Letting go of judgments.
In order to forgive, you must have judged in the first place!
You judge something as wrong because it caused you pain.
Every time you judge again you *feel* the pain.
Every time you remember, you make it wrong *again*.
The bottom line in forgiveness is to forgive *yourself* for the part you played in the scenario.

You may judge yourself wrong for not having been smart enough, or aware enough, or clever enough, to take action to protect yourself or others.

How do you un-judge?

How do you forgive yourself?

Think of yourself as an innocent child.

What advice would you give that child about how to forgive?

Put your arms around that child and tell that precious being that you love it and are taking care of it.

Put that child in your heart and give the judgment to God.

Bless that child as God blesses you.

Give the judgment to God and allow yourself to receive divine blessings.

Practice.

Keep practicing until you catch the *first thought* of judgment and give it to God so that you don't have to forgive!

Your Enormous Power

What are you creating in your inner world?

What sounds do you hear, what pictures do you create, what fragrances do you smell, what emotions do you feel?

Become aware that you are the *sole creator* of your inner world.

Think of the enormous power you have!

Regardless of what is occurring in the outside world, you are the *supreme ruler* of your inner world.

How do you choose to create your inner world?

Would you like to experience delight?

Create an interior image that brings you delight.

Make it bright, clear, colorful and life-size!

Put some sparkles in the picture if you like.

Feel the delight you have in creation.

Smile with joy.

Breathe in the sweet air that fills the atmosphere of your picture.

Let every cell in your body experience that joy.

Now become aware of what you *previously* created in your inner world.

Was it bright, sparkly, and colorful?

Do your inner creations *enhance* your daily life?

Begin now to create the kind of life you want in your outer world by focusing on what you are *already creating* all the time - *your inner world!*

෨෭ ෨෭ ෨෭

Miracle Seeds

Each loving thought contains the seed of a miracle.

Each miracle produces countless other miracle thoughts.

Loving thoughts have the power to work miracles because they are connected to God.

There is no greater force than the loving energy of your thoughts.

Terror is simply the hallucination of the withdrawal of love.

Fear is simply the identification with that hallucination.

Love is truly the *only* reality, so love's withdrawal cannot be real.

Every loving thought you have brings you closer to establishing heaven on earth.

Begin to see your world as a garden in which you are planting exquisite flowers.

This Eden is truly a manifestation of your heart's loving energy.

Your job is to keep your flowers healthy.

Love is the nourishment your garden needs to flourish.

Life, itself, is the miraculous result of God's loving thoughts.

How could it be different for you?

Aren't you made in His image?

Co-creation is simply using your energy the same way God does.

What could be simpler?

Plant your miracle seeds, one loving thought at a time, and watch paradise grow!

Manifesting Your Intention

Look at all the different forms of life.

See them as individual units of energy.

Notice how they are perfectly functioning and uniquely suited to their tasks.

Each bird, each beetle, each butterfly has the perfect design for its job.

That's why it's important to look to nature for guidance.

How does everything work so perfectly?

How can *you learn* to focus your energies so completely?

Notice how the creatures seem to perform with joy and ease.

When birds sing a song, they sing it with abandon, for the entire world to hear!

There are no half-measures in nature.

A blade of grass has only one intention – to grow!

Become aware of *your* intention.

What do you *want* to manifest?

The first step in manifesting your intention is becoming *aware* of what it is!

What is your intention?

Focus your *attention* on your *intention*.

Meditate.

Practice until it becomes effortless.

Surely you have the power of a blade of grass!

༄ ༄ ༄

The Universe, Original Sin, Creation, and You

You are a universe in miniature.

Everything that you perceive to be outside of you is also inside of you.

Infinity flows endlessly *inward* just as it flows endlessly *outward*.

That's why whatever you dream is possible.

The manifestation of your dream is already inside you.

When the energy of your dream becomes strong enough, it bursts forth as creation.

In *no place* is the glow of creation absent.

The error is not recognizing your *oneness* with divine creation.

That is original sin.

You think you exist *separately*, apart from the infinite, creative forces of the universe.

You "think."

Thinking is a characteristic of the mind.

Thinking is *not you*.

If thinking were you, you could only have *one thought,* or you would have *all thoughts* at once!

You are not your thoughts, but you can energize your thoughts with your attention.

As you energize your thoughts, you create your world.

As you create your world, you create your universe.

What kind of universe do you want to create?

What kind of universe *are you?*

Overcoming Self-Destruction

Do you hurt yourself as a reaction to *being* hurt?

The expression, "Don't cut off your nose to spite your face," means that instead of nurturing yourself, you hurt yourself *more*.

It makes no sense to deepen the damage inflicted by others, but on some level, hurting yourself involves a kind of perverted one-upmanship.

"Anything you can do to me, I can do to myself, only better (worse)."

Since outer (other) destruction is not feasible, inner destruction seems like an option.

Self-destruction occurs because it *seems* like one final way of exercising personal power.

There are many ways you can hurt yourself – through over-eating, smoking cigarettes, using drugs, not getting enough sleep, abusing alcohol, just to mention a few.

You can also hurt yourself by focusing on negative thoughts.

Hurting yourself only *seems* like a way to exercise power; it is really a plea for love.

The love you are truly seeking is self-love.

When you learn to love yourself, thoughts of self-destruction will vanish.

When you begin helping yourself instead of hurting yourself, the floodgates of love open and you realize no one can hurt you anyway!

When you begin helping yourself instead of hurting yourself, you create an armor of love which hurt *cannot* penetrate!

Next time you feel hurt, make the decision to love yourself and help yourself heal.

Breathe the Enlightened Breath

Breathe in the pure, clear, vibrant air of life!

You wouldn't have life without it.

Honor your breath for its life-giving, health-giving qualities.

The ancients have used the breath as a point of focus for eons.

In your mind's eye, follow the breath into your lungs.

As you breathe in, imagine that your breath is filled with little, tiny dots of light.

These tiny dots of light represent comfort and relaxation.

They are so small that you can breathe them into your lungs, where they travel into your bloodstream, and circulate throughout your entire body.

Breathe in the light!

Feel how good it feels to allow these light-beads to fill your entire being.

Breathe in the enlightened breath!

Fill yourself with the energy of pure, divine comfort.

Focus on your breath.

Feel the energy of enlightenment!

Your breath is a lifeline to God.

Practice.

Breathe in the breath of life!

Breathe in the earth's breath and connect with the divine light within.

Love is the Essence of Life

The essence of life is love.

Measure the success of your life not in terms of material treasures, but in terms of the love you have given to others.

Of course, love cannot truly be measured.

Love can only be *lived*.

The more you tap into the internal pool of love, the more you can express it in your daily life.

You have an *endless source* of pure love within.

No one has a greater or lesser amount.

This endless source of love is the most powerful energy in the universe.

This power of love creates life itself!

It is personal and impersonal at the same time.

Once you tap into this power, you truly understand that every single soul is worthy of love.

When you experience this deep, internal vortex of energy, individuals become adorable, regardless of their external nature.

There is no one from whom you could withhold this love.

Love's natural flow is everywhere.

You, as an individual soul, become a point, a place, from which this love flows to all others.

You become a person from which love – and life – flows.

You become an incredible blessing to others, and immeasurable blessings, naturally return to you.

How much greater a success can you be?

∾ ∾ ∾

Happiness is a Skill

Like all skills, happiness requires practice.

Like all skills, some people are better at it than others, and like all skills, almost everyone can develop it.

If you depend on something *outside* of yourself to develop happiness, you will never tap into that inner pool where infinite joy exists.

First you must *choose* happiness; like all other choices, it's an option.

The second step is to be aware that true happiness comes from *within you.*

Manifesting the perfect relationship, financial security, or achieving your ideal weight, would bring temporary pleasure, but they will not bring lasting happiness.

Real happiness can never be taken away from you.

Of course, you will experience sadness, grief and confusion at times, because that's part of the human experience, but those emotions are temporary.

Without your personal experience of sadness, grief, and confusion, you wouldn't develop the compassion and empathy necessary to help others.

Because happiness is a skill, it must be *practiced* in order to achieve it consistently.

As you practice choosing thoughts that bring you happiness, it becomes easier to put the negative states in perspective.

Decide to be happy, *no matter what!*

Practice accessing happiness and you will develop one of the most important skills in your life.

∾ ∾ ∾

Bamboo Lessons

Have you ever watched bamboo grow?

During the rainy season, the life force flows through bamboo's stalks with amazing speed.

Not only does this perennial grass grow quickly, it has incredible strength.

Each shaft emerges from the dark earth pointedly, growing straight up to the nourishing light.

During the dry season, it stands tall; it is strong, yet bends in the wind.

There is much to learn from bamboo.

Imagine all of bamboo's energy, focusing on becoming *itself!*

The stalks of bamboo are so strong that an entire temple can be built with them.

Yet at the same time, they are so flexible that they can withstand a hurricane.

Each part of bamboo has a purpose.

Its shoots can be eaten, its stalks can be used in construction, and its leaves can be used in weaving and decorating.

So much to learn from bamboo:

To be strong and yielding at the same time;

To be focused, yet delicate;

To provide beauty and nourishment;

To know when to stand still and when to grow with abandon.

Bamboo has many lessons.

Watch bamboo grow and learn!

Developing Superior Inner Strength

Superior inner strength is usually achieved through experiencing extreme or chronic trauma and turmoil.

You either develop strength or bitterness when you are forced to be strong in order to survive.

The degree to which you rise above adverse circumstances determines the degree to which you develop inner strength.

Sometimes just continuing to *live* is all that's required.

Sometimes you need to *help* others.

Sometimes you need to say *no*.

Sometimes just being *kind* is enough.

You may not think of these qualities as being strong, but it requires great strength to be kind when you are under duress.

It requires strength to *say no* to something a part of you wants to do, but that you know isn't in your best interests; to *be kind* when you feel like crying; to *help others* when *you* are in need of help; to *stay alive* when it would be easier to die.

Your life, your external circumstances, can change in an instant, but *only you* can choose how you respond.

What do you choose?

Kindness, warmth, helpfulness, love, life!

These are the qualities of superior, inner strength.

Brutality is an Expression of Self-Hatred

Brutality allows for one, small second, the experience of self-hatred to be transformed into *another's suffering*.

The pain perpetrated upon another distracts the perpetrator from his or her internal pain.

That internal pain is a result of self-hatred.

People who hate themselves fear God, because they believe God hates them, too.

They may unconsciously believe this, so they spend their lives hiding in terror of damnation.

The only way the darkness of brutality can be overcome is through the light of love.

Only love has the power to pierce the fear in which brutality lives.

Focusing on love automatically dissipates fear.

Brutality cannot co-exist with love.

It is the soul's cry for correction.

True correction is only achieved through love.

True correction is received with gratitude, and given with honor.

It is a gift from the heart to the soul.

As the heart opens, the soul can receive gifts of love and release self-hatred.

The light of love always prevails over the darkness of brutality.

Be a vehicle of love's light and the hatred in the heart can't exist.

Do You Have a Good Complainer?

Most people seem to have a built-in, automatic ability to complain.

This may seem harmless, but as you grow spiritually, you will become aware of its destructive power.

When you complain you are imbuing the situation or circumstance with even more negativity.

Complaining may seem natural, but it zaps your energy and leads you on an inner downward spiral.

Complaining is to *hell* as *prayer* is to *heaven*.

To disarm your complainer, become aware of its *first* negative thought.

Notice that the complainer is *not you*: It is a part of your *mind* that functions independently of you.

You are what is *aware* of the complainer.

As you become aware of your complainer's first negative comment, think of a word or phrase that will disarm it.

You might say something like, "Hush! You don't work for me anymore."

Say something to your complainer that will stop it from continuing, but that is not negative.

Then, in your mind's eye, visualize your complainer moving *away* from you.

As you practice this you will notice a new freedom and a new lightness within.

You will notice that you have the ability to experience joy and to share this joy with others.

As you let go of your complainer, you open the door through which true happiness and peace can enter.

Don't be zapped by your internal complainer!

If you let it, it will run (ruin) your life!

Worry is Negative Prayer

Worry is a form of *negative prayer*.

True prayer is sending blessings to others in the form of positive energy or intentions.

Since worry is based in fear, when you worry, you are inadvertently sending negative energy to whatever or whomever you are worrying about.

Worry doesn't help, *it hurts*.

Worry hurts all parties involved.

What are the pictures you have created in your mind when you worry?

Chances are, when you worry, you see other people or events in a negative situation or condition.

These internal, negative pictures *intensify* the state of fear you are already experiencing.

This causes you to go deeper into the "fight-or-flight" response, which is a state of panic.

How can this help you solve whatever condition or situation you are worrying about?

Worry only makes the situation, *and you*, worse!

Change negative prayer into positive prayer by seeing the situations or people at their absolute best.

See the people you are concerned about smiling, happy, healthy, calm, prosperous and peaceful.

This is *true prayer*.

This form of prayer *helps all* concerned.

Whenever you catch yourself in negative prayer, stop and turn it around so that you become a *helper* and not a *hindrance*.

Don't be a hindrance by sending negative prayer!

Only You Can Break Your Heart

You can only truly hate someone you truly love.

When you hate someone it may be because you're not getting what you want.

You may unconsciously think that by hating another you are setting up a protective barrier against the withdrawal of love, but that isn't so.

Ask yourself when you think you hate another, *who* is feeling that hate?

Hating does *not* keep you from hurting.

Loving keeps you from hurting!

When you feel love for another, *who* feels the love?

Hate causes the pathways of pain to become deeper.

Hate isn't real.

Hate is camouflage designed to give you the energy to recover from a broken heart.

You are breaking your own heart by *not allowing* yourself *to love.*

The secret to happiness is to love *no matter what!*

You *can* love without being a victim of another's manipulations.

You *can* love and not invite another back into your physical life.

Loving another *serves you!*

Love is a decision you make.

You *can* love unconditionally and still have physical boundaries.

You might as well give yourself permission to love, because love is underneath the hatred anyway!

Try Discipline – It's Easier!

It's actually *easier* to live a disciplined life than not.

Discipline is really a matter of implementing positive habits.

Many people's lives are miserable because they are stuck in negative habits.

Look at a negative habit as anything that causes distress in your life.

Are your negative habits helping you to achieve your ideal self?

Whatever habits you have that keep you from manifesting your ideal self are really *opportunities* for you to change.

The interesting thing about habits is that it is actually *easier* to have a positive habit than a negative habit.

A disciplined life is simply a life filled with *positive habits.*

Once you change a negative behavior into a positive behavior, and it becomes habitual, you don't have to *think* about it anymore.

It becomes automatic.

You automatically make the "right" choice.

Automatically making the right choice frees up your energy so you can be more creative, loving and productive.

You have more energy because your bad habits are no longer zapping your strength.

Discipline leads to *freedom!*

You are going to have habits anyway.

You might as well have habits that serve your highest good!

Try discipline – it's easier!

Creating Passion

What creates passion?

What stimulates your heart and your mind into movement?

Passion is the energy that connects the spiritual realms with the earthly realms and provides the impetus to create.

It generates the strength to complete your goals.

It is the result of joy that has been brought into the earthly realms from the heavens.

To discover what brings you passion, connect with what brings you joy.

Joy is the underlying force that brings life into this realm.

Passion is the energy that manifests joy into the physical.

Develop your passion and you will develop your love of life.

If you don't love your life you are wasting time in this realm.

If you don't have passion in your life now, *create it!*

Create passion by focusing on something you love.

Put your attention on one thought, idea, person, place, or thing that creates love in your heart.

Know that your love has no limits!

Let yourself love.

Allow yourself to feel love on every level of your being.

This is what creates passion!

 # Class Recordings

The following CDs are recordings from Diane's Cutting-Edge Consciousness classes.

To purchase, go to www.dianeross.com or email Diane at diane@dianeross.com.

Angel Communication	Establishing True Connections With Others
Anger, It's all the Rage	Experience the Next World Now
Becoming a Spell Breaker	Extreme Confidence
Beyond Metaphysics 101	From Powerless to Empowering
Beyond Self Esteem	Future Progression
Brain Shifting	Happiness is a Skill
Changing Your Personal History	The Heart as a Perceptual Organ
Channeling Your Higher Self	How to Increase Your Energy & Productivity Levels
Choosing Your Life	How to Re-Focus Your Energy
Cleaning Your Inner Self	How to Thrive After a Break-Up
Council of Elders	How to Understand Anyone
Courageous Souls	Increase Your Luck
Creating Inner Peace	Inner Saboteur
Creating Wealth	Instant Meditation Class
Cultivating Your Soul Center	Invoking Your Inner Sensuality
Deep Relaxation	The Law of Allowing
Deep Sleep Hypnosis	The Law of Deliberate Creation
De-stress for the Holidays	Learn Self Hypnosis
Detoxifying Painful Memories	Learning to Love Your Negativities
Discover Your Life's Purpose	
Dream Answers	Learning to Trust Again
Dream Incubation	Life Between Life
Dream Mastery	Living Fearlessly
End Cravings	
Energy Redirection Technique	

Manifesting Intentions

Manifesting Miracles

Mending Matters of the Heart

Mind Magic

Money and the Law of
Attraction

Mystical Medicine Bag

Negativity Shield

NLP Create a Shield of
Excellence

Overcoming Depression

Overcoming Worry

Past-Life Regression: Discover a
Talent or Skill

Past-Life Regression: Negative
Lessons

Past-Life Regression: To Help
You in this Lifetime

Past-Life Regression: To Serve
Your Highest Good

Past-Life Regression: Were You
a VIP?

Past-Life Regression: What do
You Want to Know?

Past-Life Regression: Your First
Incarnation

Past-Life Regression: Your Most
Honorable Previous
Lifetime

Past-Life Relationship Insights

Past Loves, Past Lives

Peaceful Mind Meditation

Personal Power

Physics of Co-Creation

Planting Inner Seeds of Growth

Primary Soul Groups

Procrastination

Releasing Blocks

Scrying

Secrets of Effective Prayer

Selecting Your Life

Solutions Through Dreaming

Soul Retrieval

Spiritual Alchemy

Spiritual Alchemy 2

Spiritual Energy: What is it, how
do you use it?

Surrender Meditation

Tap into Your Inner Brilliance

Turning Pain into Power

Understanding Your Significant
Other

From Victim into Victorious

The Voodoo Effect

What Kind of Psychic are You?

What Story do You Need to Tell?

What the Bleep Are You
Thinking?

Your Inner Healer

Your Inner Hypnotist

Your Inner Rebel

Your Spiritual Ideal

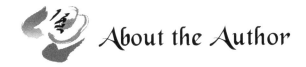

About the Author

Diane Ross's interest in altered states of consciousness began in 1970, when she first started meditating. It was at that time that she began experiencing the power of the unconscious mind.

She received her Bachelor's degree in 1971 and her Master's degree in 1974, graduating *cum laude* from California State University at Long Beach.

After teaching at high schools in California and Oregon, she entered the field of journalism and was a reporter and editor at two different newspapers in Arkansas.

In 1983 she moved to Orlando, Florida, where she currently has a private practice in hypnosis and conducts classes in meditation, hypnosis, NLP and spiritual development.

She has helped thousands of clients achieve a better quality of life in private sessions and in the many classes she teaches.

Diane has recorded more than 100 self-hypnosis and meditation CDs, which are available for purchase.

A master practitioner in NLP, she is certified through the National Guild of Hypnotists and is a member of the International Association of Regression Therapies. She is also a charter member of the Hypnosis Education Association.

Diane is available for speaking engagements and private sessions. She can be reached through www.dianeross.com, www.newyouhypnosis.com , or emailed at diane@dianeross.com.

Made in the USA
Columbia, SC
26 August 2017